UPTOWN LOCAL,
DOWNTOWN EXPRESS

JAMES STEVENSON

UPTOWN LOCAL, DOWNTOWN EXPRESS

THE VIKING PRESS
NEW YORK

First published in 1983 by The Viking Press
40 West 23rd Street, New York, N.Y. 10010

Published simultaneously in Canada by
Penguin Books Canada Limited

Most of the material in this book appeared originally in
The New Yorker in slightly different form.

LIBRARY OF CONGRESS CATALOGING IN PUBLICATION DATA
Stevenson, James, 1929–
    Uptown local, downtown express.
    1. New York (N.Y.)—Caricatures and cartoons.
    2. American wit and humor, Pictorial.   3. New York
(N.Y.)—Anecdotes, facetiae, satire, etc.   I. Title.
F128.37.S74   1983   974.7′1   82-17493
ISBN 0-670-19264-3

Printed in the United States of America
Set in CRT Caslon
Designed by Beth Tondreau

TO WILLIAM SHAWN

CONTENTS

UPTOWN LOCAL, DOWNTOWN EXPRESS

IN THE SIDEWALK

If you tend to trudge around the city with your head down, the way I do some of the time, you see a redundant landscape of filter-cigarette butts, pieces of paper, and other debris, but every so often you come to something good: one of those mini-manhole covers embedded in the sidewalk. (People who walk around with their heads held high trip over them.) Some of them, I have learned, are caps to fuel-oil lines, some are covers to valves that turn gas and water on or off, and some—the larger ones—provide access to sewers and various other pipes. They have no generic name. Since the lids are small, they generally lack the aesthetic pizzazz of their fancy relatives, the manhole covers in the street, but they often make a concise and powerful statement. Within a couple of blocks around Amsterdam Avenue in the seventies, one encounters a rich variety of sculptural works in *basso, mezzo,* and *alto relievo* as well as the timeworn *stiacciato.* The water division alone offers such forms as:

The Department of Water Supply itself has a large, distinctive plate, featuring two holes and a formal arrangement of protruding teeth.

1

Valve covers are often identified by a simple "G," for "gas."

(Some, like the above, have a metal frame around a central panel of concrete, and the initial appears to have been scooped out.)

In fact, fuel lids often lean heavily toward the utilitarian, and tend to lose excitement.

Then they overcompensate by a brazen display of self-importance, as in the Marcy Rectangular, which has a brass center.

A lot of lids give no clue to their role in society. The BPM, in the sidewalk at the northeast corner of Seventy-fifth and Broadway, provokes a reaction of uncertainty: you don't know what it can do, but you know you shouldn't touch it.

Actually, it's a surveyor's plate, and the letters "BPM" stand for "Borough President of Manhattan."

On Amsterdam, there's a lid that is flamboyantly baffling.

The puzzling "S" lid may be a monogram for the sewer system.

On the other hand, the sewer system has some perfectly explicit sidewalk lids, too.

In the inexplicable area, bold designs abound. For example, there's the Seventy-sixth Street Happel.

It clearly regards itself as an aristocrat of lids, and displays the familiar failing of snobs ("Where I come from is more important than what I do").

My particular favorite is on Seventy-fifth Street just east of Amsterdam, and conceivably it is not baffling at all—conceivably it is a crypt containing the mortal (vertical) remains of the late Mr. Chas. H. Fox—but, whatever it is, I like it a lot.

1978

GARBAGE

Most people don't much like garbage; they want it taken away—far away—preferably by somebody else and as quickly as possible. After that, they'd just as soon not think about it. At one time, the obvious thing to do with garbage was to hurl it into what has recently become known as the "environment"—mostly marshes in these parts. This method made Manhattan what it is today, but nobody likes this solution anymore. For many years Eastchester Bay, in the East Bronx, seemed to be a convenient place to put Bronx garbage—acres of wetlands became solid real estate—but that era is now over. The huge dump there, just east of the intersection of the Hutchinson River Parkway and the Bruckner Expressway, on the edge of Pelham Bay Park, has stopped growing laterally and has become, instead, a high rise. It was about the height of a ten-story building the other day, when I stopped by to take a look.

Overhead, at the top of the mountain, trucks and bulldozers were working the summit; they looked like toys, under a moving white cloud of seagulls. I strolled around the base camp—a collection of small buildings; piles of sand, gravel, and salt; construction vehicles of many sizes—as white Sanitation Department trucks streamed in, went up the mountain, and came down. Presently, Edward Sanda, a tough-looking man with blue eyes and graying hair, wearing a gleaming blue-and-gold badge and the green Sanitation cap and uniform, plus rubber boots and a buff-colored windbreaker, came by, introduced himself as foreman of the dump, and shook hands. He turned out to be a pleasant man and good company. "This is not the largest dump in the city," he said, somewhat apologetically. "That's over in Staten Island. But it's probably the highest."

"You call it a dump?" I inquired.

"Everybody calls it a dump," replied Mr. Sanda. "But the city prefers to call it 'sanitary landfill.' The reason it's so high—it's about ninety-eight feet above sea level at the top right now—is there's only eighty acres here, of which we use about seventy. It's too small, so we have to go up. There's something like five million tons of garbage here now. We work under the direction of engineers; they pick the locations and set the grade stakes." He pointed toward the top, where a huge bulldozer was pushing garbage over a precipice of other garbage, then backing up, and pushing more. "That's an active garbage bank," he said. "That's a sixty-ton bulldozer, cutting and rolling. 'Cutting' is pushing the garbage forward and down; then he rolls back, packing it. Then we spray it with either pine oil or what we call 'bubble gum'—a sweet-smelling disinfectant—and then cover it all with sand."

Sanda invited me to go to the summit, and we climbed into a white pickup truck ("This has got four-wheel drive," said Sanda) and slammed the door, on which was printed:

ENVIRONMENTAL PROTECTION ADMINISTRATION
CITY OF NEW YORK
DEPARTMENT OF SANITATION
BUREAU OF WASTE DISPOSAL

Sanda gunned it, and we headed for the foothills. "That's the maintenance shanty over there," he said, pointing out the sights. "This building is where the men can take a shower and change clothes. We've got forty or fifty men working here; it varies. We've got Sanitation men, oilers, mechanics, crane operators. The equipment ranges from earthmovers, dumpers, bulldozers, trac-

tors to a fire engine and a street flusher, which is for fire fighting or spraying disinfectant. Actually, the only way you put out a garbage fire is to bury it with a bulldozer. Over there is the electronic scale where we weigh the incoming loads. We run maybe three hundred loads a day. We accept only city garbage and private—no commercial, except by special permit."

The truck started to climb, ascending a road that went up the north face. To our left were the towers of the southern section of Co-op City. The dump appeared to block any view the occupants might have had of Long Island Sound. "They don't like us," said Sanda, "but they don't realize they're on a dump themselves. If somebody hadn't dumped there, they wouldn't be there. Anyway, when this is finished, the city is supposed to beautify it all, and get together with the local people to make it into something they can use—whatever they want."

The road turned right, and suddenly we were on top. Sanda stopped the truck and we jumped out. It was an astonishing sight: we were on a vast mesa of packed sand and garbage. Hundreds of yards off, the trucks and bulldozers were grinding away on the active bank, and gulls were screaming, but everywhere else it was quiet and empty and strange. Overhead, the sky was totally uninterrupted. The view, in every direction, was amazing. To the southwest, across the plateau, the packed garbage was almost level with the top of the gray-blue skyscrapers of Manhattan. Sanda pointed out the towers of the George Washington Bridge to the west, and the Throgs Neck and Whitestone bridges to the south. "If we go much higher," he said, "we'll be able to see the Verrazano."

We walked over to the eastern edge; a grassy slope led down to the bay, far below. "This has become a nice spot now," Sanda said. "It's an older bank. We planted some seeds, and the grass started to grow." He pointed to a low retaining wall, perhaps five feet high, at the very bottom of the slope. "I think the fill was only supposed to go as high as that wall," he said. There was a pleasant, soft breeze. "Feel that south wind?" Sanda asked. "You happened to catch a pretty nice day. We've had bad wind conditions, and trucks getting stuck in the mud. Look at the ducks swimming down there!"

We climbed back into the truck. "I was working in Rockaway before," said Sanda as we drove ahead. "They've got a dump called Edgemere. There were geese, hawks, owls, pheasants; nobody bothers them. There were wild dogs out there, too. Packs of them. They used to burrow in holes in the dump. I remember one time we found a duck's nest out there with an egg in it, right in front of where we were filling, so we postponed that area and went in a little different direction. It never did hatch. Maybe the duck sensed something.

There's not much wildlife around here. Not even rats. You could look all day and never see a rat. And very seldom at night, either. There was a strange thing at Edgemere. These old tires kept showing up. We'd cover an area with dirt, and pretty soon there'd be a bunch of tires lying on the top. I thought somebody was coming in and dumping them, but I gradually found out that that was what tires do—they sort of snake their way up through the sand, and worm their way out. They just won't stay buried."

The truck bounced and lurched over deep ruts to the southern edge, where we stopped and got out again. I noted many fragments of brick underfoot. "This was a road here," said Sanda. "I salvage stone and bricks when they come in, and use them to make a road. Then, when we get the area cut, rolled, and covered, we scrape up the road and use it someplace else. We also use crushed cans; they're very good for roads—give you traction." Sanda pointed to a couple of human figures many yards away. "See those people? We call them 'pickers.' People sneak in here and sort the material. If they find a piece of brass or anything, they take it away. We make sure they don't go where we're working, and get hurt, but otherwise it's not worth chasing them. They'll claim they're householders dumping garbage, and what can you say?" I saw at our feet, within a small space, a sweater, a plastic spoon, a shoe heel, a pink balloon saying "Happy Birthday," a rug, a milk container, lots of glass, a blue ball, a chicken leg. It was eerie to think that this was merely the most recent Cenozoic layer of garbage, and that directly below were nearly a hundred feet and five million tons of other discarded objects, mixed with sand, going down to early-1960s Precambrian. "You find money from time to time," Sanda was saying, "and several years ago somebody found parts of bodies, probably from a hospital, and I've seen many a TV set you could plug in and it would work. Nails and hypodermic needles are a hazard."

Looking over the south rim, I observed a minuscule figure in a red suit doing what appeared to be karate exercises; several people on horses moved through the park. "The mounted police have a stable in there," said Sanda, "and there's stables for the public, too. People fish over there. You see strange things from up here. One January day, it was ten degrees, and there's this woman getting baptized in the water. They didn't even have a car nearby. Just walked in—walked into the bay—baptized her, and walked away again."

We drove over to where the machines were working. The gulls circled like a slow, screaming tornado over the fresh garbage, whirling at all altitudes; the highest ones were as small as motes of dust. "These gulls will take objects and drop them on your truck," said Sanda. "I've had many a dent in the roof."

We got out.

"Watch your head," Sanda said.

He seemed to be on good terms with the seagulls, the garbage, his job—and I said so.

Sanda agreed. "Up here, it's something different every day," he said. "I took an interest. You're watching something being built." He thought for a moment, then laughed. "It's like that bridge on the River Kwai."

We walked toward the active bank.

"Every day is building here," he said. "A lot of people hate their job. You wouldn't be here if you didn't like it." He shrugged. "I've taken an interest."

Huge bulldozers were pushing garbage outward into space, where it tumbled down brightly colored twenty-foot cliffs of earlier garbage. Beyond the cliffs we could see the Palisades, across the Hudson, and, to the north, what might have been the hills of Tarrytown, miles and miles away. The nearest bulldozer shoved a mattress over the precipice, along with a tire, plastic bags, a piece of a sink, and God knows what else. "It never stops!" said Sanda, shouting over the noise. "It'll slow down, but it never stops!"

1975

8

RAINSTORM

"A violent rainstorm thundered across the New York metropolitan area yesterday," said the *Times* the other morning, "blackening the skies, drenching the ground and causing power failures, flooding and delays for hundreds of thousands of commuters. . . . The brief downpour, accompanied by wind gusts of more than 50 miles an hour in some places, dumped about half an inch of rain on midtown Manhattan within 10 minutes after it began at about 3:30 P.M." I was right on top of the story, for I had entered the Pan Am Building at three-twenty, when the sun was shining benignly, and, having conducted my business there, attempted to leave at three-forty-five by the exit on Forty-fifth Street (the one with the big columns). A whole crowd of people without raincoats or umbrellas was standing in the large open lobby staring out at the deluge. Thunder was crashing overhead and echoing off the buildings, and rain was precipitating noisily onto the pavements: *splatity-splotaty-glop-spliplaplo-plop-whooshlopita-gloop . . . Ka-ba-ba-BOOOOMM-a-boomm-mmm-mmm* (that's the thunder). The people in the shelter of Pan Am stood immobilized—errands canceled, sorties abandoned, meetings postponed—like dark statuary against the light. Life was at a halt.

Some of the rain watchers were Patient (*Illus. A*), displaying a stoic acceptance, a *que será, será* serenity, or (*Illus. B*) an I-Can-Handle-This-It's-the-Breaks-of-the-Game stance.

A

B

There were quite a few Semi-Patient (*Illus. C*) or Semi-Patient but Smoking a Cigarette Anyway (*Illus. D*), and some outright Impatient (*Illus. E*). A special case was the Deceptively Patient (*Illus. F*), a bearded man in shorts who seemed to be content, then hurled himself suddenly out into the rain and galloped down the street.

C

D

E

F

One spectator (*Illus. G*) was pensive; he appeared to be thinking large thoughts: a welcome opportunity to get it together metaphysically.

Another man (*Fig. H*) seemed simply suspended, possibly hypnotized, perhaps unaware that it was raining.

A seated man in a battered hat and wearing no shoes (*Illus. I*) reflected general indifference.

A lot of people used the lobby's columns for support, executing the Moderate Lean (*Illus. J*);

the Partial Lean (*Illus. K*);

the Full Lean (*Illus. L*);

or the Multi-
Purpose Lean—
leaning plus eat-
ing plus reading
the paper (*Illus. M*).

Some people per-
formed the Free-
Standing Eat,
such as a man
with an ice-cream
cone (*Illus. N*).

M

N

There were several Two-Person Conference Units (*Illus. O, P, Q*), who would gaze at the rain for a while, then discuss it with each other, then look at it some more.

O

P

Q

A discordant note was struck by a woman with an umbrella (*Illus. R*), who clearly had the option of going somewhere but chose not to. She created visible umbrella-envy.

R

Finally, out on the sidewalk, there were the Umbrella Haves (*Illus. S*), the carefree few who were barreling by, completing their errands, making their meetings, the rain rattling off their umbrellas, as the dry, captive Have-Nots stared at them from a few yards away.

1980

S

13

WADJABACK

One of my favorite New York words is "Wadjaback." Not too many people ever hear it, unless they're in the right place at the right time (and how many people are ever in the right place at the right time?), but those who manage to be hear it constantly. "Wadjaback" means "Watch your back," and it is shouted throughout the night by men who push handcarts at Fulton Fish Market. It doesn't mean that you should literally watch your back; it applies equally to handcarts approaching from the front or sides. A handcart pusher coming right at you down an alley of haddock will look you in the eye and say, "Wadjaback." (The danger from a fast-moving, heavily loaded handcart is not to your back, anyway—it's to your ankles. The bottom of the cart has a metal platform that supports the cargo, and its leading edge is like a dull machete. A direct hit on one's ankles from behind would probably take care of both Achilles tendons simultaneously, sending the victim briskly to the pavement and burying him under six boxes of iced flounder.) But the reason I like "Wadjaback" is that it is rather personal and specific (*your back*) as opposed to the more common New York warning (or threat) "Watch it!" where the priority is on the "it" that is about to fall on you, strike you, or run over you, and the implication is that your damn body may dent the fender of the Mack truck. In a city where people are yelling at one all the time (or being sullen, and it sometimes seems there's no in-between), the texture of a yell becomes significant. "Wadjaback" really means get the hell out of the way, but it is too polite to say so. It acknowledges that you exist—that you have a back, and that you might wish to protect it. As warnings go, it's solicitous. "Wadjaback" would be a splendid substitute for those hollow, exhausted yet challenging imprecations "Have a nice day," "Merry Christmas," and "Happy New Year." There is no nonsense to "Wadjaback," yet it combines concern, a recognition of one's humanity and vulnerability, plus good solid advice. Wadjaback!

1977

ROOFTOPS

From the window of my nineteenth-floor office, I see a lot of rooftops, and quite often, too; I generally try to fit in at least one good gaze between each major decision and chunk of solid accomplishment. The old brown wooden water tanks that perch on the roofs of the midtown area come in several styles, I've observed: (*Illus A*) The Squat; (*Illus. B*) The Twin-Squat; (*Illus. C*) The Lofty; (*Illus. D*) The Structurally Secure; and (*Illus. E*) The Exceptional, such

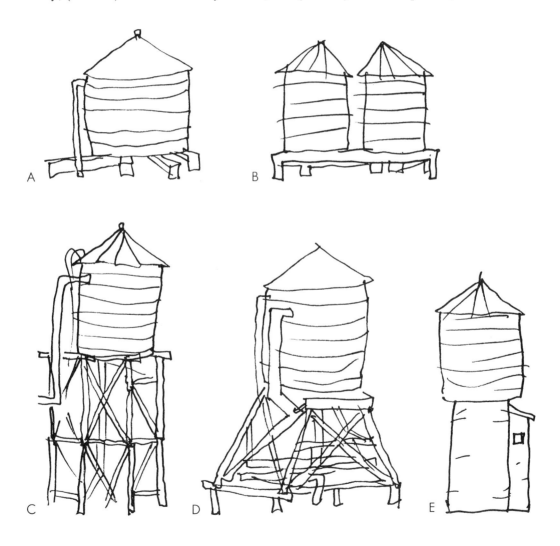

A

B

C

D

E

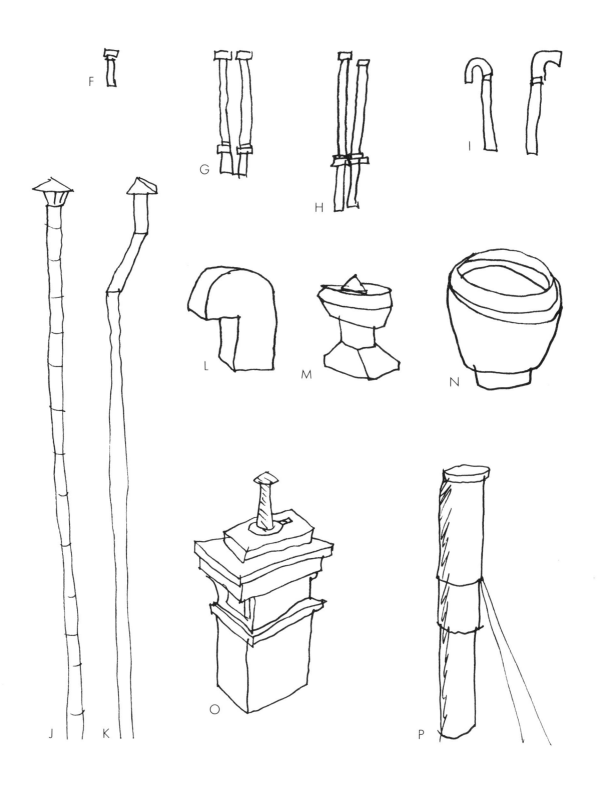

F

G

H

I

J   K

L

M

N

O

P

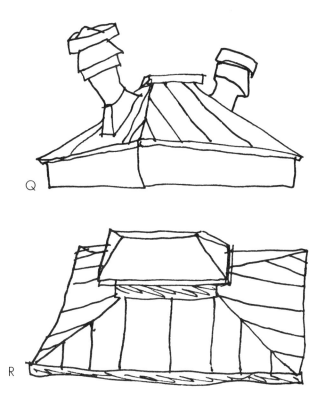

as the Combination Water Tank and Feed Granary on Forty-fifth Street. There are lots of pipes and chimneys, the most common of which is (*Illus. F*) The Solitary. This often appears in (*Illus. G*) The Equal Dual-Solitary, as well as (*Illus. H*) The Unequal Dual-Solitary, and (*Illus. I*) The Dual-Solitary Opposing-Orientation style (Equal *and* Unequal). I can see the top five stories of a (*Illus. J*) Multi-Story Vertical (with Parasol) and, nearby, an M-S V (WP) (*Illus. K*) that features a last-minute change of direction (which adds interest). A number of Cunard Line Derivatives (*Illus. L*) are visible, and a good many Jet-Engine Modifieds (*Illus. M*); less common is the large Turbo Witch Kettle (*Illus. N*). The roof of the New York Yacht Club displays a Beaux-Arts Mixed-Media Monumental (*Illus. O*) (probably one of a kind). My favorite is the Hudson River Steamboat Ordinary (*Illus. P*). Skylights abound. There is one Skylight with Twin Jets (*Illus. Q*) just to the east of me, ready for immediate takeoff; to the north is a substantial structure (*Illus. R*) I think of as the Forty-fifth Street Grime Arboretum—it contains, in my opinion, a crop of rare brown orchids that grow only in murk.

HEY, LEACH!

I was taking a walk through the old—and doomed—Washington Market area one warm and lovely afternoon last week, strolling under the dark, rooflike canopies of the ancient commission-merchant buildings and savoring the few remaining moments of this beautiful and venerable part of New York, when I first caught a glimpse of Leach and his wagon.

The out-of-town trucks were beginning to arrive, and men were unloading the vegetables and fruits, piling the sidewalks with produce. I made my way past baskets of green peppers, parsley, string beans, and cucumbers; between piled crates of tomatoes; and down corridors of boxed celery, cauliflower, scallions, and purple eggplant. The cobblestone streets were wet where ice had melted from the trucks. Above the canopies of the buildings the paint was peeling from the old brick, where the handsomely lettered names of the merchants had generally flaked and faded. Over the tarred roofs the skyscrapers of downtown gleamed in the afternoon light. I had just turned down North Moore Street—one block ahead of me was West Street and the West Side Highway and the Hudson—when I saw, between two large parked trucks, a horse and wagon standing by the sidewalk. The wagon was decrepit, having unpainted slats for sides, and huge spoked wheels with battered rims. The wagon body was mounted on stylish but rusted springs, and across its top and hanging down on both sides was a makeshift canvas cover, patched and stitched, that was partly orange and partly tan. As I approached, a small elderly man in a white baseball cap came hurrying out of one of the buildings, stuffing a piece of paper in his breast pocket, and swung himself abruptly up onto the high front seat of the wagon, shook the reins, and growled a command to the horse. The horse and wagon heaved forward and began clattering down toward the river. "That's old Leach," said a man who was sitting on a crate on the sidewalk. He watched the wagon turn the corner into West Street. "He's the last horse truck left in the market. He's been here as long as anybody remembers."

I went down to the corner, but by the time I got there, Leach and his wagon had vanished among the giant trailer-trucks rumbling down West Street.

Early the next afternoon, having asked around the market about Leach, and having been told that his first stop in the area was usually in midafternoon at a place called Bazzini's, on Park Place, I walked down Washington Street, taking my time, in the hope of finding him. The street was quiet at this hour, and nearly deserted. The day's vegetables had been trucked out during the night and early morning, and the new produce had not yet begun to arrive. The cobblestones had been brushed and washed and had dried, and only a torn leaf of green was showing here and there. Under the canopies, a few men sat on boxes, waiting, or dozed in the shadowed doorways. On one corner, a Sabrett's hot-dog man was doing a desultory business.

I turned east on Park Place and stopped at a red brick building with gray cast-iron Corinthian columns (on each of which was a yellowed metal plaque bearing a picture of an elephant holding a giant peanut in its trunk and, in small letters at the bottom, the credit VERIBRITE SIGNS, CHICAGO). Across the front of the building, just under the canopy, was the name A. L. BAZZINI CO., INC., PEANUTS, NUTS & DRIED FRUIT. Inside one of several rooms that opened onto the sidewalk, a couple of men were dumping nuts from wooden boxes into a large metal container that tapered to a chute at the bottom. I asked them if they'd seen Leach.

"Oh, *Leach*," said one of the men, smiling. He told me that Leach was due at any time to pick up some bags of peanuts.

"Old Leach," added the other man. "He'll be along."

I went out on the sidewalk to wait. In every direction there were signs of the bleak destiny that awaits the old market: to the east, the huge office buildings loomed; to the west, next door to Bazzini's, there was an open parking lot where a market building had been torn down; to the north was another parking lot, and above its car roofs I could see a third one beyond. Across from that sat a low block-long garage.

Suddenly I was aware of a sharp clatter of hooves on the cobblestones, and I turned and saw Leach, sitting very straight on the high seat of his wagon as it came rattling and lurching toward Bazzini's. Leach reined in the horse in midstreet, ignoring the cars and trucks behind him, and clambered down from his perch. He grabbed the horse's bridle and backed him up, turning, so that the wagon was parked at right angles to the sidewalk. Then he guided the horse to a position parallel to the curb, and as the traffic once again began to flow past, he hopped up onto the sidewalk. He was wearing the same baseball cap, glasses, a hearing aid, a blue coat, a checked shirt, dark pants, and blue canvas shoes with rubber soles, and he was chewing on a cigar. He untied a cord that stretched across the back of his wagon—crisscrossed between metal knobs on either side—to hold the freight in, and began dragging thirty-pound boxes of shelled pecans ("From the Land of Enchantment") down onto the sidewalk. One of the men from Bazzini's helped him stack the boxes, and then they started loading hundred-pound bags of fancy peanuts into the wagon.

19

I introduced myself to Leach, and asked him where he was going next. "Jay Street," he said. "You want a ride? All right. Get in." He indicated the mountain of peanut bags. "Sit up there." I climbed up onto the rear of the wagon and over the bags, which crunched pleasantly, and made a seat for myself on a bag just behind the driver's seat. On the floor of the wagon was a cardboard box containing oats and a honeydew melon. Leach crisscrossed the cord between the metal knobs again, guided the horse out into the street, and then bobbed up on the seat in front of me and snapped the reins. With a lurch, the wagon moved forward, and in a moment we were riding up Greenwich Street—against the traffic—with the canvas flapping like a sail above us, the wagon shaking, the springs screeching, the boards groaning and creaking, and the wheels shuddering and clanking on the cobblestones. Leach raised his hand to fend off the oncoming cars and, ignoring the honking, swung the wagon in a sharp left turn into Murray Street.

"I had a horse and wagon down here for forty years," Leach said, over the noise. "I know everybody. I'm seventy-three years old. I work when I feel like it. Half the time, I don't go out. I'm just getting by." We turned up Washington et. "I live in Brooklyn. I keep the horse and wagon on Forty-eighth Stre between Tenth and Eleventh. I take the B.M.T. over, then I come down Eleventh Avenue to West Street." Leach steered between a couple of trucks. "When this place goes, I retire," he said. "What'll I do? I won't do nothing." He shook the reins. "It's a ruination," he said. "It's going to ruin a lot of people. There's a lot closed up already." He was silent. "All my years down here, I wasted my time," he said suddenly. "I could have joined the newspaper union. I could have been retired by now. It's a new world today. I would have quit ten years ago, but I can't get rid of *him.*" He pointed at his horse, plodding along below us. "Buster, his name is."

We turned west into Jay Street, and Leach jumped down and guided Buster to the curb, pushing the wagon into a narrow space between a car and a truck. The truck was full of crates of corn on the cob, packed with ice, and the ice was dripping onto the street.

A man in a T-shirt came out of A. J. Trucco, Inc., and, after Leach had untied the cord again, helped unload the peanut sacks. "Old Leach was a big prizefighter once," said the man enthusiastically as he grabbed one end of a sack. "Wasn't you, Leach?"

Leach, holding the other end and chewing on his cigar, did not deign to reply.

I stepped out of the way of the peanuts and stood beside the wagon, looking around. Across the street, on the corner, was Joey Endive, Inc., and next to

Trucco's was A. J. Weinstein, where a man was watering some open boxes of lettuce with a garden hose. Trucks were beginning to arrive in large numbers. I stepped up onto the sidewalk and brushed against the axle of Leach's wagon, getting a large, gleaming glob of axle grease on my trousers. As I was scrubbing at it with an old mesh orange sack I had found on the pavement, a short man wearing a rubber apron came over, introduced himself as "Little Maxie from Weinstein's," offered his sympathy, and went to get a paper towel.

A trim-looking middle-aged man in a spruce business suit, spectacles, and a dazzling straw boater stepped over and expressed concern for my trousers. "I don't think that'll come off," he remarked sadly, and went on, "I'm Straw Hat Johnny Weinstein. I'm the only man in New York City who wears a straw hat three hundred and sixty-five days—or nights—of the year. I've been here in this market fifty years. You mail a postcard anywhere in the world to 'Straw Hat Johnny, New York City,' and it'll come right to me." He added, "It's true." He pointed to the building next door. "See my place?" he said. "That's the only new building that's been built on Washington Street in a hundred and fifty years. The only one. I built it in 1922." He paused. "Now it's going to be torn down, with all the rest."

"Hey, Leach!" yelled a man farther down the sidewalk. "I need a place. I got a truck coming in!"

Leach, who had finished unloading the peanuts and was now helping stack some crates of garlic in his wagon, yelled back, "When I get fifty garlic, I'll give it to ya!"

Little Maxie returned with a paper towel, and I thanked him, scrubbed up, and then, saying good-bye to Straw Hat Johnny and Little Maxie, climbed aboard the wagon again, just as Leach started guiding Buster out into the traffic.

"Were you really a prizefighter?" I asked Leach once I was settled on a stack of crated garlic and the wagon was rumbling along.

Leach muttered. "I fought about twenty times," he said, finally. "In them days, you didn't get much. Twenty-five dollars, maybe. Fifty dollars. They give you tickets, and you could sell 'em to your friends and split fifty-fifty. I was a lightweight. I fought at the Winter Garden on Grand Street. Sometimes I had to fight here in the market, too. In the old days, there was plenty of gorillas around here. They used to try to grab your customers. I'd do the best I can. I was born on Monroe Street—No. 37, I think it was—on the East Side. It's all knocked down now. It's all projects now. I went to public school there, and then I was a newsboy going through the market here, selling papers—the *Globe,* the *Evening Mail,* the Brooklyn *Standard-Union,* the Brooklyn *Eagle.* Then I was a helper in the market. You worked six days a week; you got paid

21

EXAMPLE 2. Author Jackson states that six feet of the Bronx River Parkway near Gun Hill Road "vanished" during the night of March 11, 1971. Highway authorities deny this but admit "we have no way of knowing," adding, "In any case, there's always some shrinkage during cold weather."

EXAMPLE 3. This roadside eatery stood at the southeast corner of Van Cortlandt Park until 7:29 A.M. of June 2, 1973, according to Jackson. Onetime residents of the area hold conflicting views. Some state that Howard Johnson's restaurants "all look alike," while other residents simply "don't want to get involved."

The evidence goes on. Extraterrestrial mischief? Satanic intervention? Psychokinetic maneuverings? Author Jackson suggests several hypotheses, including "soft spots" in the Bronx (some experts think that a certain patch of concrete in a field near the Hutchinson River Parkway is the actual roof of the missing Co-op City building), molecular stretch (a gradual separation of particles until they no longer form a recognizable mass; in such an instance, a Howard Johnson's would "occupy" an area of several thousand miles, and hence be unidentifiable at any particular point), and even structural-fatigue interchange, or SFI (a process believed to occur when a building, for example, can no longer "hack it" as a car wash and opts for a "simpler" existence as, say, a beach plum).

Above: Claremont Park power station.
Below: Pelham motel.

Perhaps the most frightening—indeed, devastating—piece of evidence in support of the Octagon theory was supplied by author Jackson himself. On the morning of January 3, 1974, Jackson was about to enter his garage on Tremont Avenue, prior to getting into his Volkswagen and driving to Orchard Beach to "check out a new lead" in preparation for an appearance later in the

25

day on the "Merv Griffin Show." Jackson was in high spirits, and his wife, Sarah Ann, decided to take a couple of "snaps." "It's all coming together now," said Jackson jubilantly as his wife focused the camera. They were his last words.

1975

Above: E. Powers Jackson,
8:05 A.M.
Below: 1/50 second later.

CHOCOLATES

In a bright and cheerful two-room store at 2913 Broadway, near 114th Street, a genial, gentle, soft-spoken sixty-six-year-old man named Carl Mondel has been making candy (in the back room) and selling it (in the front) since 1944. I went up to see him one cold, windy morning—the blue awning over the door, which says, in white letters, MONDEL HOME MADE CHOCOLATES, was flapping in the chill breeze—and entered the small, warm store, which smelled splendidly of chocolate. Mr. Mondel, in a tan store coat, greeted me. "Have a rum ball," he said, plucking a candy from a tray on one of the shelves of a glass display case.

"Thank you," I said. (Delicious.)

"Have a chocolate coffee cup," he said, handing me a candy in a green wrapper.

"Thank you," I said. (Superb.)

"I've counted a hundred and fifty-one kinds of candy that we make," Mr. Mondel said, waving at the crowded shelves. "Or eighty-eight, if you don't count light and dark chocolate as two kinds."

A delivery man arrived, and Mr. Mondel excused himself briefly to inquire about some gold-trimmed cardboard dividers that he needed for his heart-shaped valentine boxes. I looked at the array of candy in the display case; each tray was labeled in neat capital letters, and I noted "Butter Crunch," "Pecan Rolls," "Orange Peel," "Fudge," "French Gum Hearts," "Finlandia Marmalade," "Turtles," "Ginger," "Orange Jam," "Ginger-Lemon Jam," "Fruit Slices," "Black Raspberry Jelly," "Conversation Hearts," "Tiny Gum Drops," "Fruit Jells," "Imported Chocolate Ovals," "Tiny Jelly Hearts," "Cherry Gum Hearts," "Wintergreen & Mint," "Cream Mints," "Licorice" (all sorts), "Lentils," "Canton Ginger," "Rock Candy," "Pecan Crunch," "Cashew Clusters," "Raisin Clusters," "Peppermints," "Peanut Clusters," "Pectin Jelly Eggs," "Butterscotch Chocolate," "White Chocolate," "Cinnamon Hearts," "Nut Patties," "Kisses," "Coffee Delights," "Fruit and Vegetable Marzipan," "Dietetic Filled Chocolates," "Molasses Chips," "Caramels," "Coffee Cups," "Coffee Creams," "Orange Truffle Cups," "Vanilla Cream," "Maple Cream," "Cream Cream," "Raspberry Cream," "Cherry Nougat Hearts," "Flower Mints," "Mint Creams," "Mint Cream Dragées," "Strawberry Dragées," "Rum Sticks," and a variety of hard candies and cookies.

"When I first started out, all I knew about candy was how to eat it," Mr.

27

Mondel said after the delivery man had left. At that moment, Mrs. Mondel entered briskly, greeted me with a smile, took off her coat and hat, tied on a white apron over her dress, which was red, and went behind the glass case to get ready for the day's sales. "I've always loved candy," Mr. Mondel continued. "I always wished to have a candy shop. I came over from Hungary in 1923, and one of my first jobs was in Ohio; I worked as a packager for a company making prize packages that were sold in theaters and burlesque houses. Fifteen cents for a couple of Italian creams, and maybe a button—that was the surprise. It was too small value for the money—three or four cents' value. A gyp. Anyway, the boss had tried to make candy; he had dipped some dried fruits, like dates and prunes, in chocolate, but it hadn't worked. The more water he put in the chocolate, the harder it got. Well, there were these pots and pans lying around the loft where we worked, so, without telling the boss, I started to experiment at night, when nobody else was there, until I learned how to melt chocolate and cook candy. After four months, I finally made a candy bar that looked like the old Oh Henry! I showed it to my boss, and he was very happy. 'How many of these can you make in a minute?' he asked me. 'In a *minute*?' I said. 'It took me four months to make *this* one!' " Mr. Mondel beamed. "We made four different types of bars, and began to sell them around the Midwest."

When the prize-package business collapsed, Mr. Mondel took other jobs—working in a foundry; selling novelties and, later, insurance—but making candy remained his hobby. "About twenty-five years ago," he told me, "I began selling some of my candy to friends and relatives, and then, in December, 1944, I opened this store here."

Mr. Mondel pointed to a stack of brown cardboard cartons that were labeled, variously, "Van Leer Chocolate Co.," "Wilbur Chocolate Co.," and "Nestlé," and were piled against a display case near the front door. "These are fifty-pound blocks of chocolate," he said. "We take them in the back and melt the chocolate in a double boiler or an electric mixer." I followed him through a door that was heavily papered with children's crayon and pencil drawings ("My grandchildren did these," he said) into a small, high-ceilinged room jammed with shelves, on which were piled tins, cans, and boxes; near us were containers marked "Pecan Rolls," "Orange Peel," and "Coffee Balls," and higher up, above spools of bright satin ribbon, were cardboard boxes labeled "Halloween—Orange Pumpkins, Black Cats," "St. Patrick's Day Patties," and "Valentine 5 Lb. Hearts."

Turning a corner, we came upon a white-haired woman in a flowered apron and a green sweater who was seated at a small table, making candy. "This is Josephine," said Mr. Mondel. "She's dipping butter crunch." Josephine smiled and nodded. "The butter crunch I made yesterday," said Mr. Mondel. "Here's a tin full of it. After cooking, it is spread on marble. Then, before it's too dry, I mark it into squares with a roller cutter. That makes it easy to break." He broke off a piece and handed it to me. (Marvelous.) Josephine was also munching a little butter crunch. To her right, on the floor, was a large pot of melted chocolate. In front of her, on the table, was a piece of shiny brown paper with a puddle of the chocolate in the middle. Next to this was a pan full of ground-up nuts—a mixture of filberts, Brazil nuts, and almonds—and beyond the pan was a tray heaped with gleaming squares of butter crunch. Josephine picked up a square of the butter crunch, rolled it around in the puddle of chocolate, then plunged it into the bed of ground nuts, and laid it—now a chocolate-and-nut-covered butter-crunch candy—on a piece of paper to dry. Then she started all over again.

"We don't use any machines, except to melt the chocolate," said Mr. Mondel. "I've never even been inside a candy factory. It's all hand-done here. The chocolate has to be heated, cooled, and then heated again before it's ready for dipping. This is called 'tempering.' If I temper it twice, it's even *nicer.*"

A trim blond woman entered the back room and hung up her coat. "This is my daughter Florence," said Mr. Mondel. "She works here with me, too."

"Hi," said Florence. "My father's the best candymaker in the world."

"I don't say I'm the best in the world," Mr. Mondel said gently, "but I have a few specialties, like our rum balls, coffee balls—"

"Pecan rolls," Florence put in.

"Those *are* better than you can buy anywhere else," Mr. Mondel said quietly. He changed the subject. "Here, I'll show you some centers," he said, turning to a shelf and pulling out a tray of small squares of dark-red jelly. "These are raspberry centers. Sixty percent jam and forty percent sugar and syrup. I put twenty of them in a metal or plastic basket and dip the basket into melted chocolate. Then I shake them off, take them out with a fork, and put them on a dripping board. They dry in a few minutes." He pointed out the decorative curlicues of chocolate on the tops of some finished chocolates nearby. "We make the design on each one by dripping chocolate from a fork. It's a code. See that heart design? That means it's a raspberry cream. This 'M' here"—he called our attention to another tray—"means maple. Maple fudge, maple cream, maple anything. Orange has an 'O,' 'C' is coffee, 'V' is vanilla. These two little loops mean nougat centers."

I asked whether the Mondels themselves ate much candy.

"I'm continuously eating candy," Mr. Mondel replied. "When they"—he nodded toward his daughter and then in the direction of his wife, in the front room—"tell me to stop, I stop."

"Every day, I eat a quarter of a pound of nuts, a quarter of a pound of cookies, and a quarter of a pound of chocolates," said Florence, who is pleasantly slim. "No one's weight here has ever changed. In twenty years of selling candy, I have observed that the fat people stay fat and the thin people stay thin. Dieting has become a big fad—except for sick people, of course. For the average person, it takes away his joy. Most dietetic candy is so awful that it's a punishment to eat it. But my father's dietetic candy is good."

Mr. Mondel nodded modestly. "I make fourteen flavors," he said. He showed me a small card on which were listed, in code, about twenty ingredients that he uses in his dietetic chocolates.

"Everywhere I go, I buy different kinds of dietetic candy, to test it, and it's horrible," Florence said.

Mr. Mondel unwrapped a box of dietetic candy made by a large company. "Here's a new one," he said. "Let's see how it tastes." He took a large knife and tried to slice through one of the chocolates.

"See!" cried Florence. "He can't even cut it!"

Mr. Mondel finally cut up the chocolate, and each of us had a piece. No one spoke. Finally, Mr. Mondel shrugged.

"And that's one of the better ones," Florence said.

Mr. Mondel looked at the box. " 'Thirty-nine percent fat,' " he read aloud, and then he put the box down. "That's too much fat. I've got mine down to nine percent."

Florence pulled some red valentine heart boxes from one of the shelves. "We'll be working on these now," she said. "The candy holidays are all crammed together: Halloween, Christmas, Valentine's Day, Easter. We don't get a breath. I'm worn out. But my daughter Lillian will come in from New Jersey to help decorate the valentine hearts. She's an artist. She handpaints the colors on the chocolate bunnies at Easter, too."

Mr. Mondel led the way back into the front room. "We sell around a thousand hearts each year," he said. "I think we have the largest selection there is."

Mrs. Mondel, peering over the top of the display case, nodded.

"But we're not really enterprising," Mr. Mondel added. Then he brightened. "I'm working on my second million," he said. A pause. "I didn't make the first one," he said, smiling broadly.

"Very soon now, I'll clear all these shelves," Florence said, indicating a display case and some glass shelves along the walls where specialties of various kinds were arranged. "And then it's *all* going to be hearts!"

Mr. Mondel nodded affably.

1966

America's Best Candy

FINANCIAL FEET

On Fifth Avenue at Forty-seventh Street the other day, I recognized a young tycoon whose picture had appeared that morning in the *Times* financial section, accompanying a statement by him about a top-level shakeup in his vast corporation. Despite the bland and misty quality of his corporate patois, he made it pretty clear that he had decided whose head would roll and when, and, moreover, that his was still firmly *in situ.* Since he is younger than I am, and first came to my attention some years ago by making millions on Wall Street at about the time I was getting my first "Have You Forgotten? *Second Notice*" from my utility company, I trotted after him, staring at him discreetly and trying to figure out what—in addition to cash—he had so much of that I had so little of. His lead kept increasing until, around Fiftieth Street, I lost him completely, and my final conclusion was simply that he walked twice as fast as anybody else.

The next morning, I strode around very briskly, looking at the way people walk. In the area around Broadway and Seventy-second Street, the site of my observations, there seemed to be a minimum of fast-steppers and/or millionaires (though you never know).

The only truly executive pace I saw was shown by a high-strung black poodle, at the end of a leash. His steps were staccato and purposeful, but he never got anywhere.

A girl in brown-and-white saddle shoes was clocked at about 5 m.p.h., but for some reason I got the impression that she was not a big earner, and might even be getting money from home.

A cop with very shiny shoes was walking fast up Amsterdam, but his pace may have reflected duty rather than ambition; his income, in any case, would be fixed—subject to negotiation, of course.

An old man in space shoes was shuffling (Social Security, I hoped), and another old man—in high-tops—seemed to be following the tip of his furled umbrella, which kept eluding him on the sidewalk (I hoped he had something tucked away).

umbrella

A tall woman in gold slacks and gold high heels was doing about one click per 1.5 seconds, and I gave her a five-figure income.

People in sneakers were either running or park-bench stationary; no in-between. It is my belief that running is not a sign of financial prowess or promise; the tycoon walks fast but does not *run*. Desperate people run. Running indicates that opportunity is slipping—or has already slipped—through one's fingers. (Jogging is a different matter, although not very different.) People who are missing a bus run. People who have just stolen something run.

33

I observed quite a lot of sandals and shower shoes: low-income.

A woman in yellow high heels was charting a *lento* course down Broadway: whichever way her toe was pointing when her foot landed, that's the direction she went. She was sober but had a remarkably relaxed attitude. I couldn't estimate her pay scale exactly, but I felt that, whatever her job was, she was in some danger of losing it.

In Verdi Square, pigeons were going around at tycoon velocity, but they lacked the quiet assurance of major executives. They appeared to be over their heads in puts and calls or commodity futures. The feet that were most confident and relaxed and successful-looking were not moving at all. They were on top of a pedestal in the park and belonged to Giuseppe Verdi. He made a lot of lire in his day, and deserved them.

1978

34

HERMAN MELVILLE IN NEW YORK

A hard-rock Broadway musical of Herman Melville's somber metaphysical novel *Billy Budd*? A press-agent acquaintance of mine—one with an unusually high veracity quotient—assured me it was true; the show, called *Billy,* was, in fact, rehearsing at that very moment in an old Japanese theater on the fifth floor of a Puerto Rican movie house at Broadway and Ninety-seventh Street. I went up there directly, and found the stage hung with rigging, the crew of the H.M.S. *Indomitable* dancing below, Captain Vere pacing about, Claggart lurking in one corner, and Billy himself clinging to the ratlines. A solitary piano provided the music, and the sound was contemporary, if not outright hard-rock; the dancing was exciting. I watched for a while and then, on the way downtown, I started thinking about Herman Melville.

Melville was a New Yorker—born here (1819), died here (1891), and lived here most of his life. I began to wonder if any traces of him were left anywhere around the city, or, indeed, if any of the city he knew was still here. Not likely, I thought, but I decided to take a look. Doing some preparatory reading, I was reminded that Melville's life was a painful one, for a number of reasons. "Melville . . . suffered no less than Job," wrote Raymond Weaver. Although *Moby Dick* is one of the greatest novels ever written in the English language, the book—like all his others, except the first one—was largely ignored, misunderstood, or attacked. He was never free of heavy debt. He was a terribly complex man, torn by ambivalences. His father—once rich—died, crazed and bankrupt, when Herman was twelve, leaving behind a widow and eight children; Herman's relationship with his mother was tangled, obsessive. Newton Arvin discusses "the perilous intensity of feeling between mother and son." The boy was inculcated early with the bleakest brand of Calvinism ("that . . . sense of Innate Depravity and Original Sin," wrote Melville later, "from whose visitations . . . no deeply thinking mind is . . . wholly free"); he made a marriage that was, at least initially, agonizing; illness and sudden death were frequent in his family; he was a poor father ("These children were orphaned," wrote Lewis Mumford, "even when their father sat among them"); one son killed himself, perhaps accidentally; another ran away. He spent nineteen years toward the end of his life as a customs inspector in New York, doing menial work, and he died, almost totally forgotten, in 1891.

> Right and left, the streets take you waterward. Its extreme down-town is the battery, where that noble mole is washed by waves, and cooled by breezes. . . . Look at the crowds of water-gazers there. Circumambulate the city of a dreamy Sabbath afternoon. Go from Corlears Hook to Coenties Slip, and from thence, by Whitehall, northward. What do you see?—Posted like silent sentinels all around the town, stand thousands upon thousands of mortal men fixed in ocean reveries. —*Moby Dick*

A few days after seeing the *Billy* rehearsal, I went down to the Battery to find the place where Melville was born. His father, Allan Melvill*—an importer of French silks, taffetas, ribbons, and such—had a house at 6 Pearl Street, a few steps east of the park, between State and Whitehall streets. It was a busy district of importers in 1819, and crowded; in September, Melvill sent his month-old son, Herman, and the rest of the family off to Albany to stay with his in-laws, the Gansevoorts,† because there was "the alarm of Fever." Standing on the corner of Pearl Street, I had a fine view across the Battery, but it would have been even better in 1819: Castle Garden was still there, and the "churn" flagstaff, and the Bay and the Hudson would have been full of sails (the British blockade that had crippled American shipping was broken with the War of 1812; the Black Ball packet line to Liverpool was started in 1816) and perhaps a few steamboats (the *Savannah*, the first steamboat to cross the Atlantic, did it in 1819). Two blocks north was, and is, Bowling Green, and just around the corner was Archibald Gracie's downtown mansion (his country house is currently occupied by the Lindsay family). The Melvill house is gone, but there is a small brown plaque on the Pearl Street side of the Seamen's Church Institute—a wiggly-walled modern red-brick structure facing the Battery—identifying No. 6 as the birthplace of Herman Melville. (The plaque was put up by the New York Community Trust in 1968.) On the north side of Pearl, a thirty-five-story office building was going up, and there was a terrible din. I saw no "silent sentinels . . . fixed in ocean reveries"—just a lot of construction workers in orange helmets, wading through the slushy street.

I went "by Whitehall, northward" to find 55 Cortlandt Street, half a mile uptown, where the Melvills moved in 1820. "We have hired a Cook & Nurse

---

* The name became Melville soon after Allan's death.

† The Gansevoorts, being old Dutch, were fancier than the Melvilles, who were merely old English . . . a fact that Allan was encouraged to bear in mind; *his* father, however, was an officer in the Revolutionary War and had been an "Indian" in the Boston Tea Party. He had an unwholesome interest in watching fires and died from overexposure at ninety, after a cold night of "buffing."

& only want a Waiter to complete our domestic establishment," Allan, apparently prospering, reported to his father. I discovered that not only was the old house gone but the entire block was gone; the street itself had vanished; the west end of Cortlandt is now part of a huge reddish-brown canyon at least sixty feet deep, four blocks long, and two blocks wide. TO MEET THE NEEDS OF THE SPECTACULAR TWIN-TOWERED WORLD TRADE CENTER, says a blue Con Ed sign at the brink of the abyss, WE ARE STRENGTHENING OUR ELECTRICAL, STEAM, AND GAS FACILITIES. One of the spectacular twins, in skeletal form, already loomed at the north end, four large red-and-white cranes sitting on its

37

uppermost floor; its sibling, however, was still just a hole in the ground. There was a roar of construction noises—chuffings and clankings and garglings. East of the pit, on Cortlandt Street, there were some shabby stores—luggage, clothes, cutlery—and a bar. I walked past some large trailers (SLATTERY, AMERICAN CATERERS) and stood on the lip of the vast dig, gazing down. Suddenly, the uppermost tip of a giant crane swung by, like a metal mast, only a few yards away, its base far out of sight below. "Now small fowls flew screaming over the yet yawning gulf," begins the last sentence of *Moby Dick* (the *Pequod* has sunk). I walked away—it was too noisy to hear the seagulls—and headed uptown.

"We have leas'd a House for four Years in Bleecker Street," Melville's mother, Maria, wrote in 1824, ". . . 'tis New. . . . A handsome two Story house plan'd similar to the one we now occupy—but more convenient—the Hall is as wide, & at the end of it a Tea room . . . on entering the house, it has a pleasing effect . . . a yard—about one Hundred feet by 26—with Grass Plot & Flower Beds. . . . The Prospect extensive & pleasing . . . Those elegant white Marble Houses in Bond Street—& also in Broadway present themselves to the View from the back windows & the Bowery." Allan Melvill, who paid three hundred dollars a year for the lease, described the place as "an open, dry & elevated location equidistant from Broadway to the Bowery, in plain sight of both & almost uniting the advantages of town & country." It certainly doesn't unite them anymore, I discovered: 33 Bleecker Street is at the head of Mott Street, in a grim, drab area of large buildings whose upper floors appear empty. A gray, padlocked door in an old but undistinguished six-story building said 33, and the number seemed to include the D. & C. Paper & Twine Co. (Corrugated Cartons) and also a narrow, nameless luncheonette. Next door, at 29–31, was the Regency Sheet Metal Company. A couple of blocks east was the Bowery; I went over there—a derelict lurched down the avenue, throwing crazed salutes to each passerby—and then back west to Broadway at Bond Street, where the Melvills moved in 1828.

"We have taken a House in Broadway (No. 675—if I mistake not) for 5 years @ $5.75," Allan wrote. ". . . the Lot is 200 feet deep, through to Mercer St.—Maria is charmed with the House & situation." Mrs. Melvill seemed to feel that they had finally found something a Gansevoort could live in. It was, in her words, "a first rate 2 Story House . . . on the Fashionable side of the Street being open in Front & no buildings on that side from Bond to Jones st which leaves a delightful opening & pure air for our Boys to play. . . . Mr. Melvill playfully says I have at last gained my point which has always been a House in Broadway—My spirits are better & I am a more agreeable companion than I have been for some time past." Herman and his sister, she notes, attend dancing school.

No. 675 Broadway is now the Century Restaurant Equipment Company, a somewhat cluttered wholesale store with stacks of pots, walls of glasses and ladles, and a sample stove near the door, on the ground floor of the Broadway Central Hotel. The hotel, a stylish gray building similar to other hotels built in the 1870s, occupies most of the block; the lobby, to put it charitably, has a transitional air. Near the front door is a plaque, but not for Melville. BIRTHPLACE OF MAJOR LEAGUE BASEBALL, it says. ON THIS SITE THE NATIONAL LEAGUE OF PROFESSIONAL BASEBALL CLUBS WAS ORGANIZED FEBRUARY 2, 1876.

Two years later, Allan Melvill—drastically overextended—was wiped out. He moved his family to Albany, and took shelter there with the Gansevoorts.

Herman Melville was twenty-seven when he returned to New York. He stood about five foot nine, wore a big beard, and was quite handsome. In the interim, he had worked briefly in a bank, in a fur store, and on a farm, taught school, sailed on a whaler to the Pacific, jumped ship in the Marquesas, lived with cannibals, been rescued, and beachcombed in Hawaii; he returned on the frigate *United States* (witnessing 163 floggings during the fourteen months he was on board), and wrote *Typee,* a novel about his adventures with the cannibals. It was a popular success ("A sharp, graceful, most readable book this," wrote Walt Whitman, reviewing it for the Brooklyn *Eagle*), and Melville borrowed heavily to buy a house at 103 Fourth Avenue. In it, he installed his new wife, Elizabeth (daughter of the chief justice of Massachusetts, Lemuel Shaw), his mother, his four sisters, and two brothers (one of whom brought along *his* wife). In the next few years, Melville would have four children of his own.

No. 103 Fourth Avenue is now part of a twelve-story stone-and-brick building that shares the east side of the avenue, between Eleventh and Twelfth streets, with the Cooper Station Post Office. The door numbered 103 says: ERNEST DEFFNER/MANUFACTURERS/IMPORTERS & WHOLESALERS OF MUSICAL MERCHANDISE. Inside, packing boxes are visible. There are some old four-story brick houses across the avenue, and several secondhand bookstores. (Melville spent a lot of time in secondhand bookstores.) I went into one, and asked the proprietor, a woman, if she knew that Herman Melville had once lived across the street. "I never knew that," she said severely, and seemed to take it personally. I went into the next bookstore, a pleasantly musty old place called the Anchor Book Shop, where the proprietor, a white-haired man, was bent over a book at his desk. "Did you know Herman Melville lived—" I began, but the old man cut me off before I could get the question out.

40

"Across the street," he said affably, pointing out the window. "He lived over there." This was more like it, and I stayed for what turned out to be a very pleasant chat. "I had a customer once who knew Melville," the man said. "Name was Weglin. When he was a boy, he used to work for a bookseller, and he'd deliver books to Melville. Dead now."

In September 1850 Melville and his family moved to Pittsfield, Massachusetts. (He had written to Hawthorne of his disgust "with the heat and dust of the babylonish brick-kiln of New York.") He completed his masterpiece, *Moby Dick,* in less than a year, shortly before his thirty-second birthday. His life became increasingly bleak. "Bitter it is to be poor & bitter to be reviled," he wrote in a travel journal (his father-in-law paid for a trip to the Holy Land in 1856 when Melville appeared to be having a nervous breakdown), and to Hawthorne he wrote, "Dollars damn me, and the malicious devil is forever grinning in upon me, holding the door ajar. . . . What I feel most moved to write, that is banned—it will not pay. Yet, altogether write the *other* way I cannot. . . . Think of it! To go down to posterity as the man who lived among the cannibals. . . . I have come to regard this matter of Fame as the most transparent of all vanities."

Melville spent three years traveling around the country trying to be a lecturer, speaking for twenty or thirty dollars a night, on "Roman Statuary," "The South Seas," or "Travelling—Its Pleasures and Pains." ("In the third of these miserable winters," Newton Arvin wrote, "Melville seems to have had only three engagements altogether; and with that he abandoned his heartbreaking attempt to become a showman.") Over the years, he made repeated, futile attempts to obtain federal jobs. "I begin to indulge in the pleasing idea that my life must needs be of some value," Melville wrote in 1862. "Probably I consume a certain amount of oxygen, which unconsumed might create some disturbance in nature."

The following year, he moved his family from Pittsfield back to New York, and into a red brick house at 104 East Twenty-sixth Street, where he was to live for the rest of his life. He became an inspector of customs for New York in 1866, receiving four dollars a day, and held the job for almost twenty years. Lewis Mumford writes, "Every morning a grave, firm, square-bearded man leaves Number 104 on the south side. A little slow and reflective in gait, as if deliberately setting himself apart in pace as well as inward gesture from the world about him, Melville turns west toward Madison Square, passes through its green, and follows Fifth Avenue, whose ranks of trees are just beginning to be broken, down to Fourteenth Street . . . clear over to Hudson Street, and then turns to the block below, where the Gansevoort Market and the customs office lie, touching the river. . . . The familiarity of everything is reassuring. . . . There is a Gansevoort Hotel on Little Twelfth Street."

Both of the customhouses on West Street where Melville worked—470 and 507—have disappeared. No. 470 is a yellow brick two-story building, occupied by John S. Swift Company/ Planographers/ Photo Offset/ Printers. It faces, across the shadow of the West Side Highway, the flaking red walls of the Pennsylvania Railroad dock, a splendid relic that is still in use; through an open door we could glimpse freight cars on barges. No. 507 West Street is a Hertz-truck garage.

I walked around the Gansevoort meat market. The city put up a new market building on West Street between Little West Twelfth Street and Gansevoort in 1949—years ago, the area had been a farmers' produce market, where farmers had parked their wagons and sold vegetables in the open air—and now there are dozens of meat merchants in the vicinity. The cobblestone streets are full of trucks; men in white caps and long white coats walk about, and, under the shed roofs, slabs of butchered meat—pink, white, red, yellowish—hang from hooks. It is a noisy, vigorous, satisfying part of New York—one of those rare neighborhoods where men are doing work that is visible and specific, often with their bare hands, for a purpose that is clear and essential, and doing it in a setting of old and beautiful buildings. I looked for the Gansevoort Hotel, on Little West Twelfth, but the south corner was the city market building and the north was occupied by a two-story red-brick building that looked very old but not much like a hotel. M. KRAUS & BROS. said a sign on one side. I inquired of a couple of white-coated men who were standing by a truck in front of the building, and one of them—a young man with sideburns—said, "This *could* have been a hotel. These are some of the oldest buildings in New York."

I went inside, and upstairs—it had a nice, old pressed-tin ceiling—and in a moment I was talking to Mr. Kraus himself, a meat merchant and a most genial man, who was surprised and pleased to hear that Melville had worked in the area. He leaned back in his chair, and said, "I'm fifty-six. I'm around here fifty years, but I don't remember ever hearing this was a hotel. I do know there used to be a saloon downstairs, because my father tore it out when he bought the building, in 1923. And next door there was a piano factory. On West Street there"—he pointed over the windowsill—"freight cars used to go by on their way to Manhattan Refrigerating"—he indicated a big building visible over the rooftops a few blocks to the south—"and a donkey engine pulled the cars. An outrider—a man on a horse, carrying a lantern—rode in front. They called him the Tenth Avenue cowboy." He smiled, and then told me

42

that there are old pipes running underground all through the market, carrying brine (which has a very low freezing point) from Manhattan Refrigerating to all the meat merchants. I left reluctantly, and went up to 104 East Twenty-sixth Street—Melville's last home.

In the final years at 104 East Twenty-sixth, Melville wrote poetry in the evenings and on weekends; he rebuffed most intrusions from the outside world and read books, borrowing them from the New York Society Library, or buying them at nearby bookstores, and underscoring portions that interested him (e.g., from Beethoven: "I was nigh taking my life with my own hands. But Art held me back. I could not leave the world until I revealed what lay within me").

His granddaughter, Eleanor Metcalf, recalled later visiting his house the year before he died:

> His own room was a place of mystery and awe to me; there I never ventured unless invited by him. It looked bleakly north. The great mahogany desk, heavily bearing up four shelves of dull gilt and leather books; the high dim book-case, topped by strange plaster heads that peered along the ceiling level, or bent down . . . the small black iron bed, covered with dark cretonne; the narrow iron grate; the wide table in the alcove, piled with papers I would not dream of touching. . . . Yet lo, the paper-piled table also held a little bag of figs, and one of the pieces of sweet stickiness was for me. . . . I used to climb on his knee, while he told me wild tales of cannibals and tropic isles. . . . Part of the fun was to put my hands in his thick beard and squeeze it hard. [He used to take her on walks in Central Park.]

On November 18, 1888, Melville had begun to write his first novel in thirty-one years—*Billy Budd*. In the next months, he underscored a number of passages in various volumes of Schopenhauer ("The more a man belongs to posterity, in other words, to humanity in general, the more of an alien he is to his contemporaries"). On April 19, 1891, he wrote the last line of *Billy Budd*:

> I am sleepy, and the oozy weeds about me twist.

Five months later, at seventy-two, Melville was dead. An obituary in the New York *Press* said, ". . . even his own generation has long thought him dead, so quiet have been the later years of his life." *Billy Budd* was not published in America until forty years after his death.

I approached 104 East Twenty-sixth Street from the west, checking the numbers, and found it; 104 is the freight entrance of a fairly new twelve-story building on the east side of Park Avenue South (WILLIAM ISELIN & CO., it says across the front). There was absolutely nothing to see—just a blank doorway, exactly like a thousand other ugly freight entrances all over the city of New York. I had a sad, empty feeling of desolation—a freight entrance, not even a *place*; just a point of arrivals and departures, and of packages, boxes, not even human beings. It was a forlorn and final confirmation that nothing was left, and nobody cared. And then something on the side of the big, barren building caught my eye. Just to the left of the doorway, on a stone pillar, about six feet above the sidewalk, somebody—somebody with a crayon—had written lightly on the rough stone: "Herman Melville Lived Here."

1969

SHADOWS

The other morning, at nine o'clock—since it was a cool, splendid, sunny day—I conducted a brief study of shadows on Forty-sixth Street between Fifth and Sixth: shadows cast by the sun slanting down on the street, the sidewalk, and the sides of buildings. I found a variety of shadow types, beyond the Basic Pedestrian—a lively but familiar kind, in which humanoid globs glide across the pavement (*Illus. A, B, C, D, E, F*)—

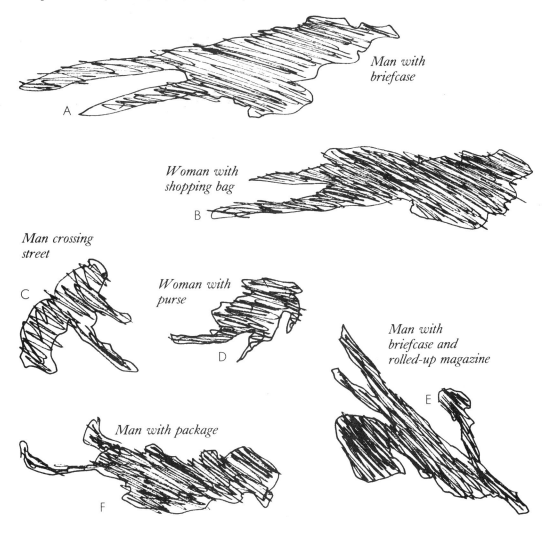

Man with briefcase

A

Woman with shopping bag

B

Man crossing street

C

Woman with purse

D

Man with briefcase and rolled-up magazine

E

Man with package

F

and the Readily Identifiable, as
seen in Lamppost (*Illus. G*)

G

and in Parked Van and
Awning of Lazar's Men's
Clothing (*Illus. H*).

H

A subdivision of the latter type is
the Two-Part Readily Identifiable,
shown in *Illus. I*—Trash Basket
(Sidewalk & Street).

46

I

More challenging shadows were
created by the air conditioner
above the second-floor windows of
Art Brite Wallpaper (*Illus. J*),

the panel truck of Vital Office Supplies (*Illus. K*),

and the revolving door at a side
entrance of 1166 Sixth Avenue
(*Illus. L*).

Similarly difficult is the Human
Still-Life Arrangement (*Illus. M*),
which requires some explication
(you had to be there): it was
created by two mailmen, one of
them sitting on a standpipe and
the other leaning against a wall next
to him, holding a mailbag. The
second postal worker's shadow is
not visible, having merged with
the shadow of the first (right), but
the shadow of his mailbag is clear.

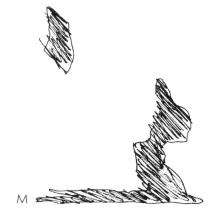

The most exciting category I saw was the Flamboyant, or Instantaneous Rorschach—a dramatic two-stage shadow sequence, shown here (*Illus. N, O, P*) in the second stage. It occurs when a pedestrian gets close to a building and his or her shadow suddenly slides part way up the wall.

1979

CIRCUS TIME

Six-thirty A.M. Cold and clear, with a challenging breeze from the Hudson. Just east of Twelfth Avenue, in a lot between Thirty-fourth and Thirty-fifth streets, low sunlight is splashing off the tops of silver railroad cars belonging to the Ringling Brothers and Barnum & Bailey Circus—about forty of them, on three tracks—which, along with a lot of silver trucks, yellow buses, trailers, mobile homes, motorcycles, and cars, arrived last night around midnight from Baltimore. The tracks curve away eastward toward Madison Square Garden, where the circus will open tonight. The only person in sight is a young photographer, taking pictures of the Ringling Brothers lettering—splendid white capitals outlined in black on a red background—on the sides of the cars. "They've already taken the cats into the Garden," he tells me. "The elephants are still boarded up. There's a parade around nine-thirty this morning."

From between trailers, an elderly woman in slacks appears, pulled along by a large taffy-colored chow on a leash. I admire the dog, and the woman says, cheerfully, "She's just about run me to death this morning," and then they are gone.

The railroad cars give no clue to their contents, except that some are passenger cars and some are freight cars—there is straw sticking out of one partly opened door—and I wonder what animals are where. The photographer passes by again, so I ask him. "There's an elephant there," he says, pointing to a freight car that has a two-foot-square window with a metal grate over it. I step closer to the car and suddenly smell the hearty, evocative, promising, and piercing smell of *circus*. Behind the grate, what I thought was an umber-colored curtain or a piece of wood is definitely elephant hide: deep wrinkles, furrows, ancient cross-hatchings. Mysterious; alien; awesome. *It moves.* I stare at it, fascinated. Then I hurry back to the avenue and into a small blue-painted diner to get warm.

It is smoky, pleasant, and crowded, and I sit next to some men who work for the circus. "I work on the maintenance of the railroad cars," one of them tells me. He is a lean, bony man with a lined face, deep-set eyes, and graying curly hair. His work gloves, oily and still holding the configuration of his hands, lie on the counter next to his coffee cup. He is wearing a stained jumpsuit, a flannel shirt, work boots, and a red wool hat with the words RICHMOND SPIDERS knitted into it. "I bought this cap in Richmond, Virginia," the man says, taking it off and examining it. "I don't know who the Spiders are."

"The Spiders are a football team or a team at the University of Richmond," says a companion.

"I didn't have this but a week before somebody cut the top off," the first man says ruefully, showing me the damage.

I ask him if he's seen this year's circus.

"Not yet," he says. "I see it once a year—usually when I get to some place where I've got relatives." He smiles. "I don't intend to see it this year until I reach California."

He lights a cigarette, and I ask him how he likes the work.

"I like it. Before this, I worked with a carnival. I was with a traveling fun house with rotating barrels. We had a forty-foot trailer pulled by a two-tank ten-speed Ford. You'd drive five hundred miles to the fairgrounds, unload, put up slippery pig-iron steel in the mud and rain, plug in the electricity, then sleep on a canvas on the floor next to the barrels, then take it all down, pack it in the trailer, and drive five hundred more miles. This is a little bit *better!*" He drinks some coffee. "On the road, you see things other people haven't seen," he says. "I like the Painted Desert, and parts of Colorado. I like between Sacramento and Reno. I like Virginia City. I guess I like northern Nevada the best of all. I've worked at every kind of job there is. I'm forty-two. I've worked at Boeing in Seattle, Washington. Worked in Reno as a busboy. Four years in the U.S. Navy. Did construction on a gold-and-silver mine. Picked oranges in Southern California. That was the worst, I guess. I was up on a ladder leaning against a branch, reaching out for oranges like this—and the branch gave way. Crash." He grinned. "I worked on an assembly line in Lansing, Michigan, where I was born in the first place. Painting around doors. That paid the most money. My father dropped dead, and I had to get him buried. When I got him buried, then I left." He pauses. "A man has to have a reason to stay put," he says. "I never had a reason to."

A walkie-talkie squawks on the counter nearby, and the man's companion picks it up; speaks, listens. It is time for them to resume work. We shake hands, and say good-bye. A well-dressed woman comes into the diner leading three small children. "What time is the parade?" she asks.

1979

TRUCKS

Gallant & Wein, Puro, Bilkays Express, Teitler Linen, Lehigh Air Conditioning, Dellwood, Bonny Box, Renofab, Hi-Vue Dairy Farms, Ryder, Hittner, Menella's Poultry, Broadway Maintenance, U.P.S., Waldorf Carting, Streit Matzoth, Consolidated Laundries, McGlynn Hays, Embassy Grocery, S & S Soap . . . The trucks clattering down the avenues, locking grids, and double-parking on the side streets of Manhattan are, generally speaking, nothing much to look at. Their business is usually stated in simple terms in plain type on the sides of the vehicle, and that's that. There are, fortunately, exceptions. Brunckhorst (Boars Head meats) has a striking truck, for example, and Zampieri Brothers Bakers presents a stylish baseball script rendered in gold on a rich red background.

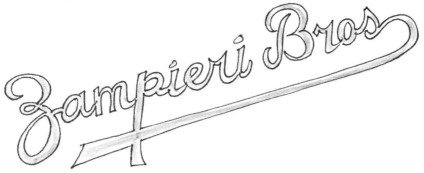

For general magnificence, however, I like the trucks of the Universal Sanitation Corporation. Five of these dark-green beauties roll through the streets at an hour when most people are still asleep; they pick up prestige slops at the Plaza, the Waldorf-Astoria, the New York Hilton, and other hotels.

Since it is difficult to appreciate fully the complex splendor of a Universal when it is moving, and moving in semidarkness at that, I went up to the company's garage, at 1381 Oak Point Avenue, in the Hunts Point section of the Bronx, to get a look at one standing still, in daylight. I met the owners, Benny Villani and Marty Sternberg, and Tom Ceglio, the foreman, and we all stood around their big garage admiring one of the trucks. It was basically a deep green—more blue than yellow—and Mr. Sternberg told me, "The city

requires private garbage trucks to be green. Beyond that, you may decorate as you choose." There were white letters with red drop-shadows; yellow letters with red lines inside them; a variety of typefaces; white pinstriping and decoration; a bold logo featuring a blue globe with a yellow continent on it—shaped sort of like South America—and a red scroll across part of it saying UNIVERSAL in white letters; and a lot of additional information here and there, including several listings of Universal's phone number (RE 4-4080).

"These trucks carry twenty-five cubic yards of garbage compacted, which would be seventy-five cubic yards loose," said Tom Ceglio. "They're 2R Leach Packmasters with a Model 600 Mack in front. They pick up an average of one and a half loads a day at each of the hotels. Conventions, of course, produce more garbage."

"The logo with the globe goes back thirteen years," said Mr. Villani. "I designed it with a free-lance artist named Al Mancuso when Sternberg and I bought the company, and that was thirteen years ago. We like an attractive, clean look."

Mr. Sternberg nodded.

The next morning, I spotted a Universal compacting at the Plaza, so I stopped and said hello to the driver, a short, cheerful man. I asked him what he thought of the Universals.

"They go good," he said enthusiastically.

"Are they the best-looking trucks in New York?" I asked.

He thought for a moment. "No," he said. "The D.V. Carting Company trucks, from Utica Avenue in Brooklyn, are better-looking."

1981

EIGHTH AVENUE

Eighth Avenue in the forties is a mean part of the city, and on a bitter, windy night it is extra sad; even the drifters are in a hurry. As I walked down the avenue one evening, the bright lights of the peep shows and porno movies seemed medical: a man in an overcoat came rushing out an exit like a patient in a bathrobe, angry-looking (malpractice? exorbitant fees? still uncured?) and almost crashed into me. I stepped to the curb. Across the street, in a mostly darkened building, some movement in lighted windows caught my eye: it was a fourth-floor rehearsal studio. The windows were steamed up because of the cold, but pale silhouettes appeared and disappeared, thin figures making arabesques: Matisse cutouts. A graceful dancer moved toward the window, hand on hip, elbow out, and perhaps she leaned against the glass because, for a moment, she was a clear, dark shape, and then she moved away, her arm describing a lovely, decisive arc as she joined the other dancers—light gray—turning in silent convolutions, working toward some kind of beauty.

1979

THE NONPAREIL

Between the Harlem River and the Harlem River Drive, just below Dyckman Street, there is a thin strip of land that gets narrower and narrower until, a few hundred yards to the south, it yields to the river entirely. An old-fashioned fence of widely spaced rusting spikes runs along the highway side, and behind this are lots of trees, through which can be seen glimpses of the river; University Heights, on the opposite shore; the Major Deegan Expressway; the shiny metal globe of the old New York University Aerospace Center; and, on the near bank—this caught my eye—what appears to be a tall, stylish Victorian gazebo rising from the roof of a grayish building.

One recent noon, I executed a flanking movement around the rusty fence, advanced into the general area through a parking lot on the north, and presently was trespassing at a leisurely pace down an old, uncitylike dirt road—parallel to the highway, and only a few yards from it—under the graceful, arching branches of tall trees. The road soon turned toward the river, and came to an end between two large gray buildings on the shore. The farther one had a sign that said FORDHAM RACING ASSOCIATION; the nearer building—the one with the gazebo tower—had a sign saying NONPAREIL ROWING CLUB 1874. This old structure—two stories high, with its open-air tower adding twenty feet more, and a tall flagpole on top of that—appeared to be authentic 1870s, all right; except for a few additions here and there, some new shingles and siding, and a certain amount of fairly contemporary paint, it looked as if it had been left pretty much alone since it was built. There was a sunken garden at the back—or so it seemed—overgrown with tall grass and goldenrod; then I noticed two posts on either side near the middle, and I realized this had once been a tennis court. Nobody was around. The upstairs windows were curtained. It was very still.

I walked along the side of the building, past a well-worn horseshoe pitch, an outdoor grill, and some upturned benches, to the front. Here, beneath the tower, a grand second-story veranda overlooked a wide, uneven, aging dock or launching platform that extended thirty yards or so outward and downward into the olive-brown waters of the Harlem River. A large black sign attached to the balcony declared NONPAREIL R.C. in red letters to passing ships and the opposite shore. Two garage-sized sliding doors flanked a narrow staircase with fancy balusters that led to the veranda overhead. I couldn't go up: a trapdoor of sorts sealed the opening above. I settled for a ground-level view of the river, and went out—very carefully—on the dock. To the south, Fordham's launching facilities appeared to be in slightly superior repair; its clubhouse, however, lacked the stately elegance of the Nonpareil. Beyond, a couple of ramshackle houseboats rested on wooden piles or cinder blocks in marsh grass. The last visible structure was a one-story building with a new-looking dock. ATA-LANTA, said a sign on the front. AMERICA'S OLDEST BOAT CLUB. I couldn't read the date. I looked to the north: a few small marinas on the edge of the parking lot, and, in the distance, looming over all, the huge Con Edison power plant, with its tall twin smokestacks.

I turned back to the Nonpareil, and realized that I was under surveillance by a slit-eyed, severely disapproving gray-and-white cat. Nevertheless, I walked over and peered through a crack of one of the big sliding doors, and saw, dimly, portions of dark oars, stacked horizontally. I moved around to the north side of the building (there was another handsome balcony here), put my nose to a window, and came eyeball-to-eyeball with another cat, this one a savage orange-yellow job. I went to the next window, and through dirty panes I saw a ghostly scene: dusty varnished racing shells and sculls around a room in racks, the long, thin hulls gleaming in soft amber sunlight. There was a workbench on the far side, and an aluminum canoe; several metal beer kegs glittered on the floor; and old-fashioned wood-slat lawn chairs sat here and there. It was mysterious and ancient and dim.

I walked toward the back of the building, and came to a large windowless wing that looked like an old icehouse; it had a single door, which was ajar. I peered in. It was a handball court: silent, empty, white. By now, a third cat—this one black—was watching me, so I walked away into the parking lot, glancing back from time to time at the old structure. An elderly man was getting out of a car near one of the marinas, and I hailed him and asked if he could tell me something about the Nonpareil.

"Oh, that's a rowing club," he said. "So's the one beyond it—the Fordham boathouse. Fordham bought the building from the blind people; it used to be a rowing club for the blind. The Fordham crew rows every afternoon. Nowadays, they've got a girl for a coxswain, too." He smiled in wonder.

"What about the Nonpareil?" I asked. "Do they race the Fordham crew?"

"*Race?*" said the old man. "They don't even row."

"Why not?" I asked.

"They're all seventy, eighty years old," he replied. "Judges and politicians." He said good-bye, and walked away to the marina.

At a gas station nearby, I found a phone booth, and looked up the number of the Nonpareil Rowing Club. Later in the day, thinking to ask some questions about the club, I started to dial the number; then, abruptly, I hung up. I really didn't want to know any more. I preferred to imagine what it was like inside the Nonpareil: white-haired, pink-cheeked, portly gentlemen with rheumy eyes, recollecting Fiorello LaGuardia and old Boss Flynn, croaking their ancient anecdotes to half-deaf cronies over cold, foamy beer, and one of them, drifting off, dreaming of an afternoon long ago when, with some of these same good friends (all young and strong then, smart as paint and full of beans), they hoisted one of the golden, gleaming shells to their shoulders, marched it out to the end of the dock, and lowered it into the sun-sparkling river.

1975

I.R.T. STOP

If you don't happen to know that the miniature Peruvian cathedral sitting in the middle of Broadway at Seventy-second Street is the I.R.T. subway station, you won't get much help from the sign. All it says is:

Baffling to anybody not into metropolitan color codes and digit cryptography. (The drive toward simplicity—originally laudable—has resulted merely in mystification of a higher order.) I like to go there anyway, just to sightsee. It is rather dim, reasonably smelly, handsomely constructed, and full of noise and activity, and there is often a pigeon on top. (X marks the pigeon.)

High up on both the north and the south façade are bas-relief shields of light blue, and these have numerals on them that can't be beat.

The frieze over the main doorway features a sturdy lamp—a five-bulber—

and, once you get inside, there are walls of white tile (tending toward the choleric) and soaring steel arches that carry the eye upward from the nave to the apex of the corrugated roof, where a row of small windows of historic dinginess provides a mellow light.

The capitals on the steel columns are stylish.

Artificial light comes from several sources, including neon lights and some simple chandeliers.

The railings of the stairs that lead passengers down to the subway itself have a certain dignity and authority. Above the doorways leading to what were once (long ago) public bathrooms are eroded-looking signs that appear to have been carved out of stone.

My favorite things of all, however, are the ancient enamel plaques mounted on the inside of the deep-brown swinging doors of the entrance. They are models of clarity. They are white with blue borders and blue letters, and their message—devoid of color codes—is simple and, to me, oddly satisfying. They say:

1978

HOUSE

Washington Market on the lower West Side used to be a quiet place by day, but, at night, when the trucks loaded with vegetables and fruit from the country came rumbling down the cobblestone streets to the four-story brick buildings of the commission merchants, it turned busy, noisy, lurid, crowded, and exciting. Each building had a black wooden awning that projected over the sidewalk, and the crates of splendid-smelling produce would be stacked beneath these. In summer, the sidewalks would be wet with melting ice; in winter, workers warmed their hands at wood-crate fires in steel drums. Within a few hours, the commission merchants would have bought and resold the vegetables, fruit, cheese, pickles, and other foods, and it would be trucked away to the groceries and restaurants of the city. The entire market emptied out and fell silent again prior to dawn.

The market was knocked down and bulldozed in the 1970s—the vegetable market moved up to Hunts Point in the Bronx—and today the area is mostly parking lots and weeds and overgrown rubble. There is a new apartment complex to the north (with a park); the World Trade Center and other large buildings to the south; some old and handsome brick buildings along Greenwich Street to the east; and the abandoned structure of the former West Side Highway to the west. Beyond that, there is landfill where Pier 19 once stood. In this wasteland of civic improvement, there is one solitary and ancient four-story red brick building still standing. It's on the corner of Warren Street and West Street—No. 179 West Street—and there is a tall weeping willow growing on the north side, a plane tree on the south, and a substantial jungle of ailanthus and lesser shrubs all around. On one side, along the sidewalk, there is a post-and-lintel arrangement of three huge stone slabs—a formal entrance leading only to weeds. It once formed the doorway to a commission merchant's building, probably, since there are faded signs and letters still visible on the vertical stone. On the doorsill of the front door (a door with many locks) there is a mosaic of brown and white tiles.

The view from the fourth story must be remarkable, I thought: a sweeping vista over and through the young saplings growing on the West Side Highway; a grand look both up and down the Hudson. There was a light in a window on the second floor, but no signs of life, and, since it was only nine o'clock on a Sunday morning, I did not knock on the door and inquire as to who lived inside and why the building was still standing. I never did find out, either, but I did hear some neighborhood opinions. The first came from a young man who was about to play tennis with a young woman on a court in the Washington Market Community Park (an INTERIM SITE IMPROVEMENT PROGRAM, said a Housing Preservation & Development sign) at Chambers Street. I asked him who lived at No. 179. "I don't know," he said, "but I hear music coming out of there sometimes, so I know somebody's in there. That building used to be McCloskey's Bar—a longshoremen's bar. But there weren't many customers once the piers shut down, so they closed it. The people who built these big apartment buildings here tried to buy that house, but the guy who lived in it just refused."

"Three cheers for him!" said the young woman enthusiastically, and they started to rally.

Nearby, there were people eating breakfast at wooden tables, or reading papers, or walking dogs. A man was working in a community flower garden, and I asked him about the house. "It's some artist," he said. "There's some guy here who knows him, but"—he looked around—"I don't see him here today."

The theory I liked best came from a couple of men in a bar on Greenwich Street. They were cleaning up from Saturday night; the stools were upside down on the bar, and, when I leaned in the open door, one man said, "We're closed."

I asked if they knew anything about the mysterious house.

"I understand there's somebody living in there, and he won't sell," said one of the men, who was wearing a red T-shirt. He peered out the window, across the weeds and parking lots, at the house in the distance. "He's holding up all the construction around here."

The other man glanced around, and then said, confidentially, "That house is not even on the city blueprints." He paused. "Officially, it doesn't even exist."

"That's why it's still standing," said the first.

"How can they knock it down if it doesn't exist?" said the second.

They both nodded.

1981

BRONX ZOO

The Bronx Zoo in bloom: breeze shaking white blossoms; pink and blue balloons bouncing on strings; not a cloud in sight; perfect Sunday afternoon. "What are they doing?" asks elderly woman on arm of elderly man with cigar, peering at heaps of earth where Sea Lion Pool usually is. Told that they're fixing everything up, she says, "Oh, that's nice. It's such a *beautiful* zoo." Prairie dogs digging vigorously next to Elephant House; men digging forty yards away at site of expanding Children's Zoo. Piles of lumber, cinder block; bulldozers, trucks; whine of electric saws and hammering over animal noises. ZOO RENAISSANCE, say signs. Crowd sauntering about (familiar sound of stroller wheels squeaking) looking for animal action. Many animals asleep. Tiger dead to world, with paw over face (*Illus. A*).

Camel and elephant rides temporarily closed, as is Children's Zoo, but Skyfari (aerial ride) is working, as is Safari Tour train (A LECTURE TOUR GIVEN BY A DRIVER-GUIDE. LEARN ABOUT WILD ANIMALS. SEE THE LATEST BABIES, says sign). Large baboon is hugging small baboon (mother and child?); both seem to have drifted off (*Illus. B*).

62

IN ORDER TO CONSERVE WATER, says sign in Reptile House, THUNDERSTORMS ARE TEMPORARILY DISCONTINUED. Another sign says, SHHHHH! SOME OF THE CROCODILES ARE BUILDING NESTS! Not at the'moment; most appear to be in REM sleep, although two False Gavials are floating snout to snout, eyes open, as if in conference. Outdoors, one otter is vigorously scrubbing himself by stream; second otter digs in earth, getting dirtier and dirtier, then runs over and dives into water for cleanup. Four wild boars are dozing, curved tusks pointed skyward. Inside Small-Mammal House (red-lit in places to simulate night), a Two-Toed Sloth is suspended from a grille by his nails (possibly catching nap), but the Suricate is definitely wide-awake (*Illus. C*).

A Spotted Skunk lying in corner of his cage looks like lump of fur, except that his stripes expand and contract. Two Lesser Spear-Nosed Bats are dangling and twitching (bad dreams?), but the Pen-Tailed Bettong ("rarely seen nocturnal marsupial" who looks like tiny kangaroo) is leaping around wildly. Two companions of mine, Kathleen and Emily (both aged twelve), catch up with me at the Great Apes (all awake), and, having just ridden the Skyfari, ask to go once more. Clearly waste of money as well as of educational opportunities. "Sure," I say. They're off. Wind lifts one feather on otherwise stationary White-Naped Crane (*Illus. D*).

D

I spot what may be Latest Baby. It is on young mother's lap, on bench, drinking milk: strawberry-patterned pajamas; pink-and-blue sweater; white wool hat and booties. Name is Melissa. How old? "She's three months old," says mother. Definitely a contender. Stroll past sleeping Pygmy Hippo and lively Dik-Dik, then see, across excavated area, bouquet of giraffes (*Illus. E*).

E

Back at Elephant House, three residents are taking walk with keeper, trunks holding tails. Kathleen and Emily appear with pink helium balloon. (Emily's was blue; it got away.) Time to leave. "Wait," says Kathleen. Tears piece of paper from brown bag containing zoo T-shirts they have bought, and writes message instructing whoever finds this balloon to write to Kathleen at such-and-such address. She ties paper to balloon string, releases balloon. It sails up and over Monkey House, disappears beyond light-green treetops, heading south.

FOUR A.M.

There aren't too many appealing places to go in Manhattan at four in the morning. The streets are desolate; the few cars that are moving seem secretive, bent on melancholy errands; pedestrians are rare and nervous-looking. Dawn is a long way off. I was driving around the city at that hour last week, stopping at stoplights that didn't matter, listening to country-western on the radio, and rummaging through the familiar trash barrel of my mind, plucking at ratty memories, poking at old wounds inflicted or received, sorting out yearnings, examining the imminence of doom—the usual dog's breakfast of rumination. It was, in addition, damn cold: you could feel each and every bone in your fingers. I drove through places that I used to like. Washington Market, years ago, would be just ending its day around this hour, still smelling great, with bits of celery and lettuce on the wet cobblestones. (Kaput.) A sign on the World Trade Center (which did the old market in) was lit, boasting the view from the hundred-and-seventh floor. Of what, I wondered. The really

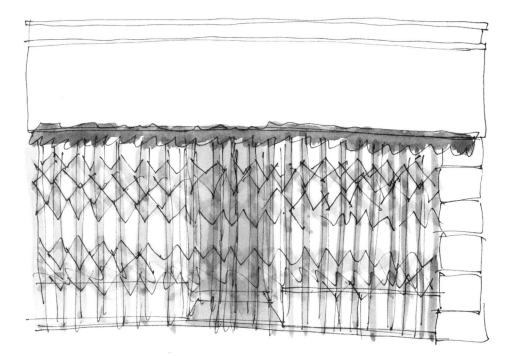

good thing to see was gone. I went around Battery Park; spotted a fireboat in the darkness (that was nice); huge new office buildings, such as American Express (not nice); then swung down Fulton Street toward the river, and parked. The old fish market was full of light; flames jumped from bonfires in oil cans, cinders flying crazily, into the night sky; there was the rumble of trucks; men shouting; the clatter of dollies; boxes thudding on the pavement. Bundled-up men in rubber boots moved about, interweaving with the trucks and dollies; nobody bumped into anybody. Nobody seemed angry; everybody seemed to have a role with enough to do but not too much, and time to make a wisecrack or hail a friend. The smell was rich and splendid. The fish, extracted from the sea, had reached the next stage here: packed fin-to-fin on ice in boxes. The boxes were being put on dollies, wheeled down the grimy pavement, hurled into trucks. In one crowded shed, a colossus of a fish was lying on its personal bed of ice. "What's that?" I asked a stocky man who had a cigar butt between his teeth. "Grouper," he replied, around the butt. "Three hundred pounds."

"How did you get it in here?" I asked.

The man removed the cigar from his mouth, and replied, "With a crane." He was very pleased with his answer.

Farther down, a man called to me, "I got porgies; I got blues!"

"Just looking," I said.

A huge man in a tattered windbreaker selected a skinny black fish from a box, picked it up, and studied it. Then he put it back, and took a billfold from his hip pocket. He opened the billfold, and counted the money in it.

At a place with oysters and clams and mussels, I stood and listened to the sound that a big bag of clams makes when it is dropped on the pavement. It is not easy to duplicate (*kah-chunk-ka-ch-ch-nk?*), but it is worth listening to.

A man standing by several enormous, smooth, black-skinned tuna—decapitated and de-tailed—was periodically shouting "Hey!" in a cheerful voice to nobody in particular. It seemed to be the opening part of a sales pitch, but since nobody was around he never completed the commercial. But he appeared content.

Not far away, some small fish had fallen out of a box on a dolly and landed on the ground. Men danced around, crouching, swiftly stabbing the escapees with sharp hooks, and flipping them back into the box.

"You want shad?" asked a man in the shad area, addressing an elderly buyer.

"Nah," said the old man. "I got shad yesterday."

I went out on the dock behind the market and exchanged a few words with some crewmen who had just about finished unloading the catch—white plastic bags of scallops—from the *Felicia,* a boat fifty or sixty feet in length, painted orange above the hull, just in from ten days off Long Island. In a long shed on the other side of the dock, a black man stood on an elevated platform surrounded by huge blocks of ice—blocks suitable for building pyramids. There was a machine for grinding the ice, but the business day was coming to a close.

It was still as cold as a tuna on ice, so I went across South Street to a parked truck that sold coffee, and bought a cup. The hot cardboard warmed my fingers superbly, and I walked over to the biggest bonfire I could find. It was in a metal oil drum that had slits and odd-shaped openings around the bottom so it glowed like a Halloween pumpkin. Three or four men stood around it, throwing on slats of wooden crates and cardboard boxes. The fire roared upward, the flames almost reaching the East River Drive, overhead. A yellow dawn was starting, behind the Brooklyn Bridge. I edged toward the warming fire, and hoped the day would not arrive too soon.

1977

WHITHER WESTWAY?

Dunster Associates, Inc., a Cambridge research-analysis group that specializes in urban planning, has come up with two viable alternatives to the controversial and costly ($1.16 billion) Westway project. Mayor Ed Koch says, "They are both very nice. I like them and I don't like them." Governor Hugh Carey is reported strongly in favor of both.

AIRWAY

Airway would cost only a fraction of Westway, according to Dunster Associates, and would restore the ten-cent subway fare, set off a boom in real-estate air rights, and permit construction of at least three new convention centers. Airway's six lanes of lightweight snap-on aluminum sections—supported entirely by festive helium balloons imprinted with I LOVE NEW YORK—would whisk traffic over the city at an average height of eight hundred feet, with eye-opening alternate routes around the Empire State Building, the Chrysler Building, and the World Trade Center. Scenic overlooks, rest areas, and Howard Johnson's snack bars are planned atop the Pan Am Building, the Metropolitan Museum of Art, and Bloomingdale's. Funding would come from HUD, I.C.C., the Federal Highway Administration, and NASA.

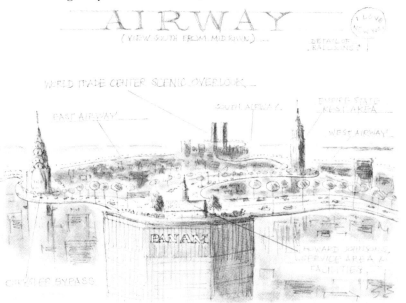

RIVERWAY

New York City's most valuable real estate, says Dunster, "is currently underwater, sitting idle under the Hudson River." An obvious solution is to "get the river out of there, move it to a more appropriate area, maximize usage of the resulting dry land, and revitalize the mud in a major way." Riverway calls for construction of two dams across the Hudson—one at Forty-second Street, the other north of Battery Place—and draining the area in between. Picturesque café-lined canals would carry the Hudson up or down Twelfth Avenue and other streets, depending on the tide (*Illus. A*).

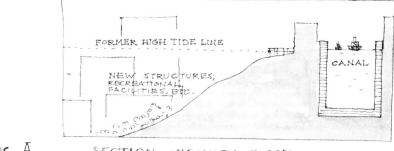

Illus. A   SECTION – VICINITY OF 28TH STREET

MR. GALISI'S STAND

On the north side of Eighty-second Street, just east of Columbus Avenue, there's an old gray wooden structure sitting on the sidewalk, up against a building. It has a blue awning in front, wire mesh over the windows, and rusty padlocks on the door. A blue sign at one end says LADIES & GENT'S SHOE SHINE AND REPAIRING.

I peered in through a dusty windowpane one morning last week. The place seemed both abandoned and preserved. Rising from a broad marble step were curving brass footrests with worn brown leather tops, where customers—ascending to sit on a green-covered bench and hoisting their pant cuffs—had once positioned their wing tips for improvement.

On the back of the
bench was a row of
small mirrors, and
tucked away beneath
the bench, on the marble
step, were bottles, rags,
cans of polish, a wrench,
and brushes of many
varieties.

Framed pictures and photographs
hung on the rear wall: Enrico Caruso;
Michelangelo's *Pietà;* Richard Tucker;
a reclining Aida, or possibly a dancer;
Beverly Sills; the Bay of Naples, with
Vesuvius smoking.

On one windowsill lay a small furled American flag, with a tassel hanging down. The room was glowing with subdued, harmonious colors: brass, brown leather, black-bristled brushes, rags that had absorbed the hues of shoe polish, dark wood, pale marble like old melted snow. Things were where they had been left; they had an air of finality and repose. As I was looking in, a passerby stopped. "Poor Mr. Galisi died last spring," he said. "This place was here when there was a Ninth Avenue 'L' stop on the corner." The man stared inside. "Mr. Galisi used to have Primo Carnera's shoes," he said. He stepped back and held his hands two feet apart, in the manner of somebody describing a fish. "They were that big."

1980

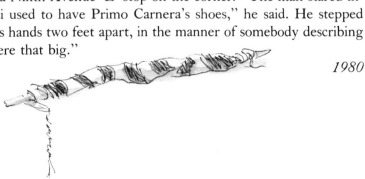

73

PLUMBER'S TRUCK

Walking around the other day, I came upon a jaunty old red pickup truck parked outside a building where some noisy renovation was going on. The truck was an International with battered, bulbous fenders, and, to judge from some shiny copper pipes sticking out from under a greasy tarpaulin in back, it belonged to a plumber. A ladder and a coil of rope hung from one side. I took a closer look: in the truckbed were faucets of various styles; a pail; loops of tubing; an acetylene tank; clamps; valves; a vise; a can of boiler putty; a wrench; lots more pipe of assorted kinds and sizes; and a great deal of stuff concealed by the tarpaulin. Two 5-foot-long wooden boxes were mounted on either side, but I don't know what was in them. (They were locked.) In the cab of the truck, there were papers attached to the sunshades by rubber bands; other documents were stuffed into a crevice above the door on the passenger side, and a fat coil of wire hung like a necklace from the rearview mirror. A pouch made of gray adhesive tape was attached to the dashboard near the speedometer; it contained eleven yellow pencils. Next to this, a cluster of nuts and washers dangled on a wire loop. On the dashboard, the seat, and the floor were deep, uneven layers of supplies and equipment. The topmost items included a drill; a flashlight; a box labeled DEEP CUTTING HOLE SAW (USE QUICK CHANGE ARBORS); a tin of grease; a box of Plumbers Abrasive Cloth; rolls of insulated wire; rolls of tape; tubes of sealant; soot remover; adhesive caulking; a screwdriver; a gray wool hat; light fixtures; paper cups; a box of Worm Drive Clamps; an oil can; a folding rule; a can of Off!; batteries; clamp lamps; and bolts. As I walked away, I thought about the tools of *my* trade (a typewriter; paper; sometimes a phone) and I felt deprived.

1979

PIERS

What is probably the most complicated and spectacular outdoor metal sculpture in New York stands at the edge of the old New York Central railroad yards on the Hudson River in the sixties. From West End Avenue, it looks like a zeppelin that has crashed or a collapsed roller coaster. It is actually the steel-beam and corrugated-iron remnants of a three-hundred-foot-long, forty-foot-high pier that burned down half a dozen years ago, leaving a rusty skeleton listing into the river. I went to take a closer look one morning. Having entered the yards at the south end, near the Con Edison plant, I climbed over one of several long concrete unloading platforms and then headed north under the elevated West Side Highway. There was a steady hum of cars, and an occasional *ba-bump* as they passed over a certain joint or pothole overhead. Along the waterfront were low mountains of trash—chunks of concrete, cardboard boxes, bags of garbage, pieces of lumber and wallboard, torn-out windows, and dirt—with weeds and tall saplings growing out of them. The pier itself was huge, rust-colored, and ghostly. Seagulls flew across its dark geometry. After a while, I turned back. A tall man in a down jacket and cowboy boots was sweeping one of the platforms. He gave me a friendly wave, and I talked to him for a bit. He told me he had worked in the area for the last ten years. "That old pier was beautiful inside," he said. "It had old-fashioned

offices, and all the rigging for the ships. It's too bad it's gone." He looked out at the river. "Farther up the shore there," he said, pointing north, "is what's left of a floating bridge they used in moving freight cars from barges onto the shore. They raised or lowered the bridge according to the tide. I used to make balsa-wood models of it and sell them at flea markets. I've probably sold fifty of them over the years. Part of that bridge is still standing. Want to take a look?"

A few minutes later, we were climbing around on the remnants of the old floating bridge, stepping over holes and jumping from beam to beam. It was a mysterious mixture of elements—mining operation, railroad trestle, and ferry slip. There were enormous wheels and winches; pipes, cables, girders; small huts, railings, charred timbers, smokestacks, stairs; and train tracks descending into the water. "This was a wonderful place," the man said. "When I was a kid, I used to hang out here with my friends. Now it's all burned and falling apart, but it's still beautiful. About once a week, a van drives up here, and a bunch of people get out—Japanese, I think—and they all start taking pictures of this."

1982

AERIAL

Most Manhattan buildings are solitary islands with limited possibilities for pedestrians. People walk in from the street, go up, go down, walk out again—that's about it. But a few buildings offer an extra dimension: they are connected to a neighbor across the street by an aerial passageway—generally an enclosed bridge. These alternate routes come in various sizes and architectural styles. Bloomingdale Boulevard, which crosses Sixtieth Street between Lexington and Third, is a good example of the simple, straightforward, and dull (*Illus. A.*). Shadowy forms occasionally move behind its murky panes. A larger version, in brown, can be seen eight floors above Twenty-fourth Street, uniting 1107 Broadway with 200 Fifth Avenue at Madison Square. It has twenty-four windows and a park view. An important-looking bridge in the S. S. & D. category is the Charlie-Wally, a dark, modern-style passage across Thames Street at Trinity Place, which enables people inside the N.Y.U. Graduate School of Business Administration to get from Charles E. Merrill Hall to C. Walter Nichols Hall, and vice versa. A two-decker S. S. & D. connects a couple of buildings at the intersection of Pine Street and Pearl Street (*Illus. B*). One of the buildings contains a United States Post Office. (The bridge could be used by post-office employees who might wish to carry the letters up to the sixth floor of their building, over to the seventh floor of the adjacent one, then up to the eighth floor, back across the bridge, and down to the post office before sorting.) There's a stately Beaux-Arts

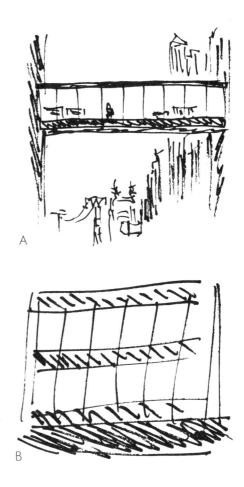

A

B

C

D

E

F

G

overpass high above Exchange Place, between the handsome old First National City Bank building that faces Wall Street and the office building at 22 William Street (*Illus. C*). Only a block away—just downhill from the New York Stock Exchange—but at the other aesthetic extreme, a silvery, futuristic mezzanine-level tube joins 20 Broad Street with 30 Broad Street (*Illus. D*). Both are stock-exchange buildings. The Metropolitan Life Insurance Company has three buildings between Twenty-third and Twenty-fifth streets. One was once the world's tallest skyscraper; the two others are joined across Twenty-fourth Street by an impressive Art Deco bridge with stainless-steel panels and sculptured windows (*Illus. E*). One of the rare passageways that cross an avenue—Lexington, in this case, between Sixty-seventh and Sixty-eighth—is Hunter College Highway, which is still under construction. It will have two major arteries, which, in the event of a funding shortfall, could be joined to create a new office building. The most magnificent structure remains the Gimbels bridge (*Illus. F*), which stands astride Thirty-second Street between Sixth and Seventh avenues, and is the Chartres of aerial tunnelry, with lots of windows, columns, panels, medallions—all sheathed in copper that is turning Landmark Green. One of the pleasantest interbuilding suprastreet traverses is some twenty stories above Broadway just north of Trinity Church and Trinity Churchyard: an elegant open bridge that goes across Thames Street from the roof of the United States Realty Building to the roof of the Trinity Building (*Illus. G*). On a hot August day, it must offer a delightful stroll—brief but breezy—for the weary cleric or the realtor in need of refreshment.

1982

HOW TO WALK AROUND NEW YORK IN A SNOW EMERGENCY

1. The only portions of snow to be trusted are those that are shallow, dark, and icy-looking (*Illus. A*). They should be nearly sidewalk-color—a deep, mottled grime with bits of lettuce or gum wrapper *en gelée*—indicating that this is no unpredictable pile of melting slush; this is snow that has opted for the life of the city, and wants very much to be pavement.

A

2. Avoid the smooth, snowy expanse that extends out into the street. It is an illusion. The surface is as delicate as a *crème brûlée*. The pedestrian who steps out onto it will instantly disappear, and the surface will quickly resume its tranquil former self (*Illus. B*).

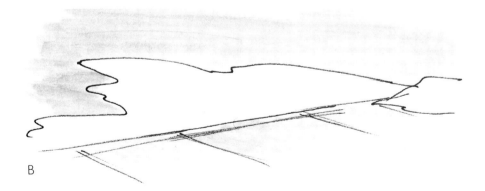

B

3. Do not attempt to cross a snowbank. If there is no alternative, try to find a path somebody else has made. Make sure the path doesn't stop in the middle. Don't experiment. You will sink in up to your waist. Then what will you do? There is no single answer. Reflection and introspection are possibilities. Wave to people. Do you know a poem by heart? (*Illus. C.*) Make a mental list. *Do not struggle.* Even if you escape, you will lose at least one shoe, and then have to continue your journey in a wet sock.

LOVELIEST OF TREES, THE CHERRY NOW IS HUNG WITH BLOOM ALONG THE BOUGH...

C

WHAT TO DO WITH A WET SOCK

Hang it over the radiator. Do not have guests in until you have removed the sock. Two socks on a radiator is one thing, but a single sock says flatly that your life needs work (*Illus. D*).

1979

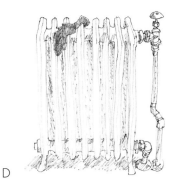

D

HUNTS POINT

The old Washington Market was a nice place to walk through late at night or very early in the morning—full of clatter and wonderful smells, towering crates of fruits and vegetables, beautiful old brick buildings, ice melting on the cobblestones—but it got torn down, and its replacement—Hunts Point Market—is a different story. Set on the desolate shoreline of the southeast Bronx, the market is huge and uninviting, surrounded by high fences of corrugated metal topped with barbed wire; guard booths block the entrances. I drove around it at 5 A.M. one morning last week; all I could see were the tops of long, stark, government-type buildings and a lot of trucks.

Outside the fence, there was little life going on: a couple of prostitutes stood silhouetted by a bonfire on a side street; the sky was funereal, with a wash of sickly green showing through a crack in the clouds to the east, where the sunrise ought to be. Hunts Point Avenue, under the streetlights, glittered with broken glass; on either side were businesses like Hunts Point Auto Wreckers—Late Model Parts; Ecuador Auto Wrecking; Mexico Auto Glass (*Instalado Mientras Ud. Espera*). At the intersection with East Bay Avenue, facing the market, there was an empty lot with a big sign announcing HUNTS POINT SERVICE CENTER. It said that Anthartz Enterprises were now leasing bank offices, medical facilities, truck maintenance, gas station, retail shop, restaurant, motel, fast food, and related services IN ACCORDANCE WITH MASTER PLAN OF CITY OF NEW YORK. In the darkness, behind the sign, I saw only tall weeds, the back seat of a car, garbage, and a lot of bottles.

I looked westward. Two more prostitutes were standing like statues in the middle of a dim street; huge trucks rolled by. When I reached Garrison Avenue, near the Bruckner overpass (and a billboard saying HELP KEEP HUNTS POINT CLEAN), I saw a couple of lighted places, so I stopped and parked. I glanced into the Tropic-A-Go-Go Snack Bar—men hunched over a long counter—then went next door to Moshman's Garrison Bakery (ALL BAKING DONE ON PREMISES), whose window had a pink-and-yellow neon coffee cup with blue steam rising from it. There were display cases of cakes and pastries, and around the upper walls were oil paintings (camels in deserts; Moses with tablets; an amiable nude). Most of the customers sat apart from one another at small tables, drinking coffee and staring into space, but at one table a couple of men were talking to each other, so I sat down not far from them—grateful to hear some voices. "When the shoe is on the other foot, that's when you really

82

feel it," one man was saying. He was a slight, mustached Puerto Rican of about forty; he wore a blue checkered cap, a wool coat, jeans, and work boots. His companion—a tall black man in a blue jacket that said NYCHA TENANT PATROL—nodded. They drank coffee and smoked cigarettes, and talked about vacations. Tenant Patrol told about the time he had taken his family to Jamaica.

I half listened, still feeling the sad, dull weight of what I had seen at Hunts Point: master plans, barbed wire, broken glass, and bonfires; human beings shivering through the night on the chance they might get bought. "I was thinking of going on a trip myself," the smaller man was saying. He began talking about visiting his old home in Puerto Rico. "All year, the town is asleep," he explained to his companion, leaning forward, "but on Christmas Eve it comes alive, and you go to this house"—he began pointing this way and that with his finger, marking an invisible street on the table—"to *this* house . . . to *this* house . . . to *this* house, and they're playing music in the street!" He sat back. "Christmas there," he said, "is really *Christmas.*"

1977

BELMONT STAKES

Did you know that Steller's sea cow (*Hydrodamalis stelleri*) "was abundant in the Bering Sea and off Kamchatka and the Aleutian Islands when it was discovered in 1741. All that is known of it comes from Steller's description, and from various museum skeletons, for it is now probably extinct. It was very like a dugong . . . but . . . considerably larger, reaching a length of twenty feet. Its skin was peculiarly rough and crinkled"?

There is always something—when you are looking up something else—that is a lot more interesting. I was not looking up sea cows or dugongs; they just happened to be next to "Horses" in my Larousse *Encyclopedia of Animal Life,* and horses—"Odd-Toed Ungulates of the Order Perissodactyla and the Equidae Family"—was the subject of my investigation the other Saturday morning, a preparative activity prior to attending the 103rd running of the Belmont Stakes. I have little knowledge of, or affection for, horses (I have been kicked by them, bitten by them, stepped on by them, and thrown from the tops of them), and I would just as soon see the 103rd swimming of the Dugong Derby as see the Belmont, but I do like events, and I have to take what is available or stay home. (The events offered in this area on Saturday were a crafts expo, an energy fair, and a skate-a-thon.) What I learned from Larousse was: "Horses, asses, zebras . . . are monodactyl, the functional digit being the middle one. . . . Bucephalus, charger of Alexander the Great, was a tridactyl, or three-toed, recalling the immediate ancestor of the horse, the late . . . Pliohippus. . . . The different parts of a horse's limbs must be clearly understood. The upper parts . . . down to the elbow or knee, are enclosed within the outline of the body. The visible parts of the legs begin with what correspond to our forearms and shins. Thus, what is commonly called the knee in a horse is really the wrist, and the equivalent posterior joint, the hock, is really an ankle. The next bone, the cannon bone, corresponds to the metacarpus or metatarsus. The pastern joint is between the foot and the toe. . . ."

This means, I realized, that if a man were to race against a horse—in a fair race—he would have to "run" lying down, balanced on one knuckle of each hand and foot, "racing," that is, with his wrists, forearms, shins, and ankles only (*Illus. A*). The horse would have a clear advantage in such a contest, but you have got to give the horse a lot of respect for running like that in the first place.

84

ILLUSTRATION A

A Fair Race

Horse

Man

"The horse's teeth," says Larousse, "are of the greatest interest.[1] Along the front of both jaws is a row of six cutting incisors called the middles, intermediates, and corners. Between these and the premolars is a space (diastema) where the bit is placed."[2]

[1] The author does not make clear whether he means of greater interest than any other part of the horse, or just plain all-time global intergalactic interest, in which case we should perhaps take this with a grain of salt.

[2] This makes it clear why the racing of horses is so much more popular in this country than the racing of cheetahs, which are a lot faster—"the fastest land animal over short distances," according to Larousse—and splashier in appearance, what with the spots and all. I had previously thought that cheetah racing failed primarily because of jockey apathy, but now I believe it is because nobody wants to find out if cheetahs have a diastema. But back to horses.[3]

[3] Well, not quite yet. "Horned toads"—which appear on the same page as "Horses" in my dictionary—"have been seen," Larousse says, "to shoot tears of blood a distance of several feet at an adversary. When the animals are very excited and 'angry' it appears that their blood pressure rises rapidly, rupturing the capillaries in the conjunctiva of the eye."[4] (*Illus. B.*) (A horned toad is actually a lizard.[5])

[4] This is clearly not an attractive social gesture, yet it seems to me an enviable talent under certain circumstances.

Once I'd learned all there was to know about horses, I drove out to Belmont Park. I left my car at the far side of the racetrack and walked around toward the finish line. It was an overcast day, windy but very hot. The huge grandstand, across the green infield, was jam-packed, even though the first race had not yet begun. I was walking along the outside track—a beautifully raked and brushed dirt track that looked like somebody's favorite window box—separated from it by a high hedge of privet and a wooden rail fence, when I came to an opening in the hedge and saw a red-and-white pole with a gold ball on top ("¼," said numerals on the side of the pole) and the homestretch beyond. What a good place this would be to see the horses go by, I thought, when, abruptly, there was a soft, rapid thumping noise, and five horses (brown, black) came galloping past the hedge, bodies elongated and stretching, legs reaching, hooves digging, dirt flying up, the jockeys—blotches of bright color—bent flat over the manes, striped arms whacking away with whips, and the sound of the hooves muffled by the deep dirt but still audible—or maybe only felt, like heartbeats—and the horses leaned into the last curve, bunched together, and tore away down the homestretch.

1981

---

[5] Lizards are more interesting to look at than horses. Male iguanas, anoles, and flying dragons have dorsal crests, dewlaps, and neck lappets—none of which you will find on Pleasant Colony. "Contrary to one of Darwin's hypotheses," says Larousse, these features have little appeal for the females, who don't have them, don't want them, and don't even want to look at them. Chameleons, incidentally, are "capable of moving their eyes independently, which greatly facilitates defense and hunting of prey." (Not to mention making them a lot of fun at parties.)

Illustration B
Horned Toad (in a good mood)

TANGO PALACE

Among the last remnants of ancient Broadway razzmatazz are the neon signs and lettered windows of the Tango Palace, on the second floor of a four-story building on the west side of Broadway at Forty-eighth Street. They must be forty years old, at least. There isn't much neon left in the Times Square area—it has been replaced by illuminated signs lit from within—but the Tango Palace still displays elegant spaghetti-curls of the old style, and also white letters on black glass windows, which surely spelled sophisticated hot times to visiting firemen and undergraduates of the thirties. It's doubtful whether anybody tangos at the Palace now—if anybody ever did—but it is a stylish ghost, and I always look up with pleasure at its dingy dignity.

1979

PROTECTED TREES

When, on a recent soft, promising, springlike morning, I took a walk on the Upper West Side in order to see the neighborhood trees bursting into bloom, I could not find a single green leaf—pinnate, palmate, lanceolate, ovate, spatulate, obovate, or quinquefoliate, of any lobation, venation, or attachment whatever. (A lot of buds, sure.) But rather than go to the office and work, I continued to stroll around, observing the various kinds of constructions used locally to preserve, protect, and defend the young trees along the sidewalks. The most common sort of protection, it appeared, was the Low Romanesque Repeating Hoop with Partial Overlap, to be seen on the south side of Seventy-fifth Street between Central Park West and Columbus Avenue (*Illus. A*). The tree that this fence was installed to protect had either just left or not yet arrived.

A taller, more elegant version of this repeating hoop pattern was visible in front of the Beresford apartment building, at 211 Central Park West: the Haut-Croquet, Painted Black (*Illus. B*).

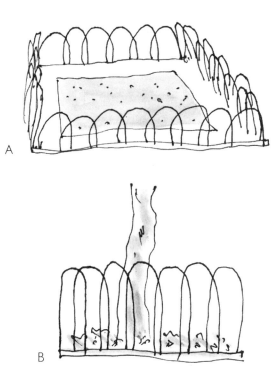

A

B

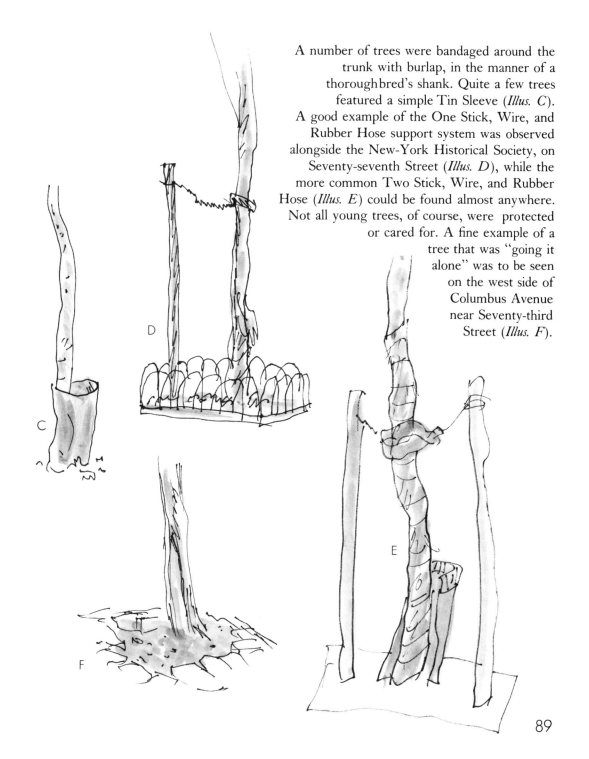

A number of trees were bandaged around the trunk with burlap, in the manner of a thoroughbred's shank. Quite a few trees featured a simple Tin Sleeve (*Illus. C*). A good example of the One Stick, Wire, and Rubber Hose support system was observed alongside the New-York Historical Society, on Seventy-seventh Street (*Illus. D*), while the more common Two Stick, Wire, and Rubber Hose (*Illus. E*) could be found almost anywhere. Not all young trees, of course, were protected or cared for. A fine example of a tree that was "going it alone" was to be seen on the west side of Columbus Avenue near Seventy-third Street (*Illus. F*).

C

D

E

F

Maximum protection was afforded by the Medieval (*Illus. G*), a metal barricade reminiscent of prisons, birdcages, and those paper pantaloons sometimes stuck on lamb chops. The most elaborately defended tree I encountered was at 11 West Seventy-fourth Street (*Illus. H*), featuring a Medieval and, in addition, an entire fence of wrought-iron curlicues and spears. Yet the forbidding structure seemed to have served as a challenge to some anonymous but passionate citizen: study of the tree trunk revealed that there had been carved—about a foot above the topmost bars—one word: *JEAN*

1981

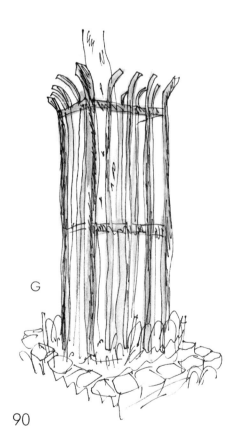

OFF OFF BROADWAY JOURNAL

July 9. Hot night in country. Ninety degrees. Trying to sleep; can't. Gypsy moths keep landing on face. Around 10 P.M., drift off into half sleep. Wakened by wrong number at ten-twenty. Toss; turn; toss; turn. Can't get back to sleep. Decide to read. Moths flutter around light. Pick up bedside copy of *Jane Eyre*. Jane, newly arrived at Thornfield Hall, is having rough night:

> . . . I started wide awake on hearing a vague murmur, peculiar and lugubrious, which sounded, I thought, just above me. I wished I had kept my candle burning: the night was drearily dark; my spirits were depressed. I rose and sat up in bed, listening. The sound was hushed.
>
> I tried again to sleep; but my heart beat anxiously: my inward tranquility was broken. The clock, far down in the hall, struck two. Just then it seemed my chamber-door was touched; as if fingers had swept the panels in groping a way along the dark gallery outside. I said, "Who is there?" Nothing answered. I was chilled with fear.
>
> . . . [There was] a demoniac laugh—low, suppressed, and deep—uttered, as it seemed, at the very keyhole of my chamber door. The head of my bed was near the door, and I thought at first the goblin-laughter stood at my bedside—or rather crouched by my pillow: but I rose, looked round, and could see nothing; while, as I still gazed, the unnatural sound was reiterated: and I knew it came from behind the panels. My first impulse was to rise and fasten the bolt; my next again to cry out, "Who is there?"
>
> Something gurgled and moaned. . . .

Scene not conducive to sleep for Jane, me, or Mr. Rochester (whose bed is presently set ablaze by the crazed woman who has escaped from the attic). I turn off light; try to think serene thoughts. At last . . . slowly . . . sink into welcome sleep. *RNNNG! RNNNG!* Reach for phone; knock over lamp; *Jane Eyre* falls to floor. "Hello?" Enthusiastic voice identifies self as Joe Steele. (Who?) He is ebullient: the play is all set! (Play?) He and playwright want to see me on Tuesday in N.Y.C. for reading—Don't worry, you have the part; no problem; we just want to see you—and he talks about how great play will be; what fun; what wonderful people. "See you Tuesday!" he cries; hangs up. I am totally awake. Clock says eleven-fifty. No chance of sleep now, and many drearily dark hours until dawn.

July 10. Morning. Call Frank in New York to tell him the news. Frank, who is not an actor, either (he's an artist), is old friend. A couple of years ago, an acquaintance asked him if he'd like to act in Off Broadway play. Frank—faced with several deadlines on work he didn't want to do—said sure. He had the time of his life; loved every minute; has never stopped talking about it. He was excellent in the play, too. After that, he got small part in movie, and now has begun to think of himself as actor who draws. Two months ago, Frank and I were walking down University Place, ran into Joe Steele, who had been in play with Frank. Steele is wiry, dark-haired young actor-director; lots of energy. Frank and Joe elated to see each other. High-velocity show-biz conversation ensued: How's Sally? Seen Howie? Liz has a part in such-and-such.

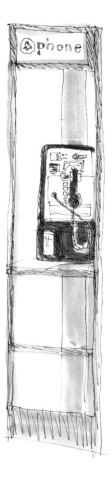

Tony's doing a commercial; Shirley's in a soap. They share laughs, reminisce; then Steele says he's going to direct an Off Off Broadway play, and wants some non-actors in cast. "Will you be available, Frank?" Will he! They continue to talk. I step forward inconspicuously; clear throat. Talk goes on. I nudge Frank. "How about him, too?" says Frank generously, finally. Steele looks me over. (Should I mention I played Lieutenant Raleigh in high-school production of *Journey's End* in 1944? Died at end of play; deeply moving. Both my parents thought I was very good.) "Want to be in the play?" Steele asks. Certainly, I reply. Good, says Steele, he'll be in touch. Dashes off. Frank excited now; back to his true calling. We walk down street feeling life is about to become less routine, boring. New directions; bright lights; late nights; beautiful actresses; cheering audiences. Reminded of scene in Walt Disney's *Pinnochio* where naïve Pinnochio goes rollicking off with bad companions, singing, "Hi, diddley-dee—an actor's life for me . . ."

JULY 14. 5:30 P.M. Next to doorway on Great Jones Street where we are to meet Steele and Allan Walters, the playwright, at six, a drunk has dropped himself on sidewalk and is shouting curses at passersby. Excellent projection: remarks reach us across street with perfect clarity. Actor? We get coffee at Phebe's, bar-restaurant with big windows, on corner of Bowery and East Fourth Street. Wonderful view uptown: big brown building containing Joe Papp's theaters on Astor Place; Empire State Building beyond. Frank grim, nervous about reading. (Why? He's done this before. Maybe *I* should be nervous. Begin to get that way.) We return to Great Jones Street—drunk has departed—and get cheerful greeting from Steele and Walters, an affable man in a rumpled pink seersucker suit. Rehearsal room is two stories high. Floor taped to indicate stage. No set. Long table; chairs. Steele and Walters chat with Frank; shoot appraising glances at me from time to time. I begin to brood: How did I get nerve to come here? Who do I think I am? What if I can't handle role? Should I back out now? Humiliation looms. Too late to quit: Steele is handing us scripts. They have black covers with small plastic windows. (What should I concentrate on? Voice? Diction? Posture? Characterization? Motivation?) Open scripts to page 56. Frank's part is MAN WHO TELLS STORY. Steele says to me, "You're ANOTHER." He and Walters beam. "Ready? Read." Frank starts reading his part aloud. It goes on and on. Suddenly I have a line:

ANOTHER: *No!*

I say it, Frank continues. Presently, I have another line: "No!" again. Then Frank resumes. Story unwinds. Finally, I have a bigger line: "My God!" Frank goes on. Turn page. Where's my part? My part is over. Frank's story ends; MAN WHO TELLS STORY and ANOTHER exit. Steele and Walters are nodding and smiling, delighted with our performances. We do it again. "Very good, very good," says Walters. They shake our hands; give us Xeroxes of the pages of the play we're on (we don't get scripts); explain rehearsal schedule; and we are out on Great Jones Street again. Walk in silence for a while. Frank says, "My part in the last play was a lot better than my part in this one." What's he complaining about? Now I am committed to daily rehearsals, then performances five nights a week for the rest of the summer, all in order to say, "No! . . . No! . . . My God!"

JULY 15. Country. "No. . . . No. . . . My God!"
   "No! . . . No! . . . My *God!*"
   "No! . . . NO! . . . MY GOD!"
   "NO! . . . NO! . . . MY GOD!"

JULY 17. Country. Party on somebody's lawn. Talk to distinguished actor. He has deep, resonant voice; exquisite diction; beard; handsome; moves well. (Are these qualities necessary?) He is waiting for writers' strike to end; will then go to California and do thirteen weeks of series for TV. Later in evening, woman I am talking to points out how the actor is now sitting in chair at one side of lawn and is backlit by garage floodlight; a silhouette with halo around him, and light coming through fringes of beard. We go over; she tells him he looks very dramatic. "I know," he booms. "That's why I'm sitting here."

JULY 18. Have told all my friends that I'm in play. Reaction I seek is congratulations; what I get is incredulity. Restless for rehearsals to start. Repressed thoughts keep bubbling up: How come Frank's role so big, mine so small? What if he gets hurt, sick . . . killed? "Tragic about Frank. Lucky thing you were around to step into the part." Went to see play at nearby summer theater. Studied acting techniques. Some actors good, some not so good. Encouraged by performance of one actress who got big audience response with only *one line.* She said her line, then gave weird giggle. Small things like that make stars. Drove home after play. "No! . . . No! . . . My God!" (Pause. Giggle.) No. Can't use it.

JULY 19. Interview in *Times* with actress Swoosie Kurtz. Read it avidly. "I work from the outside in, which is not to say I work externally." Hmm. Can't decide which way to work. " 'It's whatever works for you,' she said with a shrug." Feel better.

JULY 20. New York. Late afternoon. Having burger before first rehearsal. Outside windows of Phebe's, a couple of Hell's Angels roar by; a girl with orange hair walks past (she wears white pants and a green T-shirt with an alligator on it); a young man with a blue Mohawk haircut; a bearded codger in an old tweed sport jacket, a pink straw hat with an I LOVE N.Y. hatband, fuschia pants, carrying a black plastic garbage bag. . . . The derelicts pass, too, heading toward or away from the Salvation Army a couple of doors downtown, or the city shelter around the corner, or the bars between. Some walk sidewise with eyes closed, veering this way and that; some have torn shoes; others are barefoot; white-bearded and wrinkled; young and gaunt; bloodied; bandaged and unbandaged—it is a continuous parade of wounded veterans, limping back from private wars. Goya. Hieronymus Bosch. Maybe actors and derelicts share discomfort at being who they are. The actor, however, hopes to become—at least briefly—somebody else. The derelict has a more modest goal: he just wants to destroy himself.

JULY 22. Some scenery has been moved into the rehearsal hall during the morning, and now we stand at an actual bar. I have no problem with my lines, but I am not comfortable. I lean on the bar with my left arm, then worry about my right arm. It has nothing to do. It just hangs there stiffly. Don't know where to put it. I feel the audience will begin whispering to each other ("Psst—look at him. Wow, is he self-conscious!" "Who? The one with the arm hanging there?"). I ask Steele what to do to relax. "Don't worry about how you stand," he says. "Think about what you're feeling as Frank talks. The action will follow naturally. Don't *indicate* what you're feeling, though; just feel it. It'll be fine." Steele says we have the advantage of looking and sounding like non-actors, and we should make the most of it. "I was rehearsing in a play once and the director told me to turn upstage. I started to do it, and he yelled at me, 'No! Not like an *actor*—like a human being!' "

We talk for a while. Steele keeps reassuring Frank; tells actor stories. Rehearsals and real performances are very different, he says. Tells about actor who was in medieval play. During rehearsals, stage manager called out, "Cannon!" and actor was supposed to say, "Hark! The cannon fires! His Majesty arrives!" Worked fine during rehearsals. "Cannon!" "Hark! . . ." But on

95

opening night, there was the actual sound of cannon firing. The actor jumped, shrieked, "What the fuck was THAT?"

We resume. Frank improves. Steele and Walters give me two more lines: another "My God!" and a "My God! That's incredible!" It feels like a soliloquy.

JULY 28. Discussion of costume for play. Steele says I should have "kind of a slob image." He is distracted by other matters, but presently turns back to me, looks me over. "Why don't you just wear what you've got on?" he suggests, not unkindly. (A few days ago, I was walking down the Bowery when I saw what I thought was a college classmate drive by. He didn't see me—or maybe he did. I glanced at reflection in window: I was wearing old T-shirt, dirty pants, sneakers, no socks. At this very moment, classmate probably telling old friends, "Guess who I saw shuffling along on the Bowery?")

JULY 30. Afternoon. Driving into New York for first full-cast rehearsal. Anticipatory; preoccupied. Passing car on highway, I notice that the driver is giving me wary look. Realize I have been exclaiming, "My God! That's incredible!"

The real actors are friendly, cheerful, optimistic; generous about amateurs in their midst. We all shake hands. Rehearsal moves along. In the middle of scene I realize I'm supposed to be on the other side of the stage. Start to cross. But somebody is speaking his lines. I freeze, stuck in middle of stage like a scarecrow. Terrible sensation. Next time, I cross sooner. We run through play again. This time I can't remember whether my first "My God!" is just "My God!" or "My God! That's incredible!" Total confusion. Frank still getting his lines wrong. When he gets into trouble he increases his speed, contracting the story so there is no place for me to say, "No!"—much less "My God!" Rehearsal ends. Everybody in high spirits. Great sense of sharing in something.

AUGUST 4. Wandering around before rehearsal. On Houston Street, a used-clothes store with its door open, and a window heaped with shoes of all shapes and colors; piles of clothes inside, coats and suits and trousers—autumnal, as if blown across the avenue by a cold October wind and whirled through the open door into this dim storefront. Nearby, two legs are sticking out from a doorway: worn shoes, once black; pants the color of the sidewalk; a dirty hand hanging over one knee. The hand recedes; vanishes; reappears clutching a bottle of bright-red liquid. The bottle rises; disappears. The legs, the doorway, the pavement—everything has a wash of dirt over it, toning down the colors. Except the bright-red drink.

Between Lafayette Street and Mulberry Street, a derelict lies sleeping in a shadowed alley; two large red-brick buildings rise on either side, with metal shutters (many open) on every floor. It is an area of large, fat, proud old buildings—their shutters like flags or kites; festive—and their strength and solidity contrast sharply with the skeletal, ragged men lurching among them now. Some of these men speak—mutter, growl, rasp—but they are not speaking to anybody in particular. They speak to the world at large, like actors.

AUGUST 6. We go to the real theater tonight. Frank has been reading Stanislavski, he says; very helpful. The block on which the theater stands is shrill with portable radios; kids yelling to each other; people shouting down from fire escapes; dogs barking; cars honking; garbage cans clattering. Teen-agers sit on hood of car, hugging and kissing; old people sit on stoops of the tenements, fanning themselves, playing cards, speaking Spanish. Children are skipping rope; throwing balls; weaving through crowded sidewalk on roller skates. Frank steps over man who is passed out on sidewalk, and, entering theater, says, "It would be hard to do a play in here that could compete with the human drama out there." Theater is in big, dim, musty building; go up wide steps to second floor; through another door; sign in; go around side of bleachers; down dark passage; and then—abruptly—there is the nearly completed set, brightly lit, and the other actors. Greetings to all, and rehearsal begins. Frank has not yet learned his lines, and is very nervous. Every time he skips a cue, I lose a line. Since I have only ten words in toto, I resent losing any of them. Eight words, I now feel, is my absolute minimum, I won't do it for seven. When, on the way out after rehearsal, I say to Frank, "Damn it, why can't you learn your lines?" he looks at me as if betrayed, clearly thinking, This is the person I helped to get a part?

AUGUST 7. The set is finished; looks great. Mike, the designer, is also the builder and painter. He has worked like hell, carrying heavy materials up the long flights of stairs into the theater, where the temperature is steadily in the nineties, regardless of what the weather is outside; he's built the set, then painted it to make it look real and old. He gets little help, and demands no credit; just does it. A genuine professional. Rehearsal goes well; late in evening, everybody goes to Phebe's. One by one, the actors stop at the table where Joe Steele is sitting; tell him how well the show is going. Steele listens; agrees pleasantly. Then, invariably, each actor adds one qualifier: "Of course,

97

So-and-So isn't loud enough," or other comment. Steele is amused by this. He is a skilled diplomat, among other things; he must get along with the actors, shape their performances without damaging their morale. Steele tells me I am fine. (Fine? Is that better than OK?)

AUGUST 8. Rehearsals getting more intense. Steele has been working with actors during the day; then full rehearsal at night; he's beginning to look slightly haggard. Tonight we went into rehearsal around six. It was a very hot, sticky, sunny afternoon. Five hours later, we came out into a dark downpour of steady rain. Nobody knew it was raining. There is little or no sense of outside world when we are inside theater. Increasingly, this theater and the play in it are becoming the real world. (Yesterday I was watching somebody walk down the street, and thought: That's a very good walk; very convincing.) We sit on folding chairs behind the set, waiting to go on. The stage is bright—lit from the front and above—but where we sit is shadowy; the actors are dim shapes. It is a kind of limbo.

It's hard to go home at night, and, once there, it's hard to sleep. When the main rehearsal is over, we all stay and watch others rehearse special bits. Everybody's tired, but they don't want it to end; they don't want to miss anything. When, finally, there is nothing left to see, the actors drift over to Phebe's, drink beer, and let down slowly. Some of the actors are old friends; have worked together before. They joke about how they have gone from Off Off Broadway play to play, never getting money or fame. What matters is to be doing a play, some play, and trying to do it well. They make ends meet as best they can—unemployment; a part in a soap; an occasional commercial; odd jobs in between. They have a lot of admiration for each other, a lot of generosity, and great love for their work. They respect one another's professionalism. Joe Steele talks about an actress called Irene. They were in a play together a few years back. Irene had a scene with an actor named George, and it was very funny. Irene managed to get five separate laughs out of the scene each night. Then George had to leave to be in a movie, and he was replaced by another actor. This actor gave a different reading to the role, and now Irene was getting laughs in completely new places: eight laughs a night. Then George finished the movie, and came back to the play. "You know what Irene did?" says Steele. "She got George to change his original reading so that she got thirteen laughs every night—the original five plus the other eight." He slaps the table with glee. "She's *great*!"

AUGUST 9. Three days until opening. Went to American Museum of Natural History; saw Shakespeare show. Globe Theatre, it turns out, was situated in much crummier part of London than our theater is in N.Y.C. (No bear-baiting halls on Bowery, for example.) Museum had filmstrips of actors doing Shakespeare, including young Olivier as Hamlet. "Alas, poor Yorick," says Olivier, gazing at skull he holds in hand. Then—totally surprising move—Olivier turns to Gravedigger (offscreen) and remarks, "I knew him well." Then turns back to skull; continues. Made me laugh: it was so fresh and right.

Near the theater, in early evening, a skin-and-bones derelict comes out of the municipal shelter for homeless men, moving stiff-legged as if on stilts; goes to the edge of the sidewalk. Stands there awhile; plods back; returns again. He repeats the process over and over, as if the edge of the sidewalk were a lookout, a vantage point, a place where he is able to gaze into some sort of distance—perhaps to see something coming, something he expects.

"I'm going to give you a sixty-second lesson in acting," says Steele, when I get to theater. He wants me to speak louder. He has Mike, the stage designer, stand at the bottom of the stairs of the bleachers. "Say your line to me," says Steele, "but make it so Mike can hear it." "My God! That's incredible!" I say. "OK," says Steele. "Mike—go up a few steps." Mike does so; I repeat my line. We do it again, as Mike moves up to the highest reaches of the theater. "MY GOD! THAT'S INCREDIBLE!" "Did you hear him, Mike?" asks Steele. Mike says yes. "Good," says Steele to me. "Now you know something about acting." Rehearsal proceeds. Frank is doing very well. At Phebe's afterward, attractive and skillful young actress describes how she spent three years as a waitress in N.Y. before she got any parts. Another talks about how she was lucky to find theater work in Vermont. Steele says, "The hardest thing in the theater is writing. Then comes acting. Then producing, and then directing." Not sure he is serious, but maybe. He talks about one of the other amateur actors in the cast, who is getting lots of admiration. "He's never acted before," says Steele, "but once we open and he sees the power he's got over a roomful of people, he's not going to want to go back to what he usually does." It's going to be hard for everybody to go back. What were evenings like when nobody had to be at the theater at seven o'clock? What was life like? We have all become quite close, without knowing very much about each other. The actors greet each other with waves, kisses, embraces, handshakes, laughter. Would people in any other line of work be so open, so affectionate? Don't know.

AUGUST 12. Opening night. Joe Steele addresses cast. "I think you're ready," he says; wishes everybody luck. Cheers and applause. Dan, the stage manager, announces the time at intervals: "Ladies and gentlemen: Half hour." "The audience is entering the house." "Ladies and gentlemen: fifteen minutes!" Frank is sitting in a corner, saying his lines over and over. He has been giving good performances, but he still worries. "Places!" calls Dan. The house lights go down. Chairs creak. A few coughs. Then silence. Beyond the dark set, the lights come up onstage; the voices begin.

SEPTEMBER 7. Country. Gray day. Flat, dull light; no sun. Very quiet. The play ended a week ago. Mike, who built the set, has dismantled it. The actors have dispersed. Frank is back to drawing pictures and meeting deadlines. The last party at Phebe's was noisy, touching, and fun; talk of reunions, and phone numbers written on soggy napkins; hugs and kisses; then, we all separated for the last time. Most of the phone calls will never get made; the reunions will never take place; in fact, we will probably move further and further apart until names are no longer remembered, and then the faces will vanish, too—but it seems unlikely that any of us will forget the short, good time when we were a company of players, and brought a play to life. Finished *Jane Eyre* last night; she married Rochester. "We entered the wood, and wended homeward."

1981

WAKING UP

Waking up in an apartment on the upper West Side on a November morning, with the day invisible but damp, feeling yesterday recede and wondering about today, hearing a garbage truck whining over its breakfast on a street nearby, I raise the yellowed window shade. It rattles upward, and reveals backyards and puddles, bare trees, brick houses, the black silhouettes of water towers, chimneys, TV aerials. Against the backdrop of a brown apartment house, light-gray smoke is emerging steadily, diligently, from a stack on a roof below. Once it rises past the brown building, the smoke is no longer visible; while I slept, it filled the sky.

1977